Purpose Driven Martial Arts

**KARATE FOR CHRIST
INTERNATIONAL**

**INSTRUCTOR / SCHOOL
CERTIFICATION MANUAL**

Written by Dr. Daryl R. Covington

With essays and ideas contributed by
Michael Mason, Michael Lewis, Joseph Lumpkin, David Dunn, Steven Riggs, Leslie
Sowl, Mark Barlow, Chris Dewey, Fariborz Ashahk, Donnie Bryson, Kang Rhee,
George Petrotta, Donald and Char Englehardt,
David Sheram, and Erle Montiague

Purpose Driven Martial Arts
KARATE FOR CHRIST INTERNATIONAL
INSTRUCTOR / SCHOOL CERTIFICATION MANUAL
Copyright © 2006 Daryl Covington

Fifth Estate Publishers,

Post Office Box 116, Blountsville, AL 35031.

First Printing 2006

Cover art by An Quigley

Printed on acid-free paper

Library of Congress Control No: 2006935251

ISBN: 1933580313

Fifth Estate 2006

ABOUT THIS BOOK

This book serves a guideline to help Karate for Christ member schools and instructors become certified with our organization. It also serves to aid them in their ministry. You are welcome to use the ideas within this book whether you follow through with the certification process or not. It is our prayer it will aid you in your ministry.

A BRIEF HISTORY OF KARATE FOR CHRIST INTERNATIONAL

Karate for Christ ministries began in 1955 as an evangelistic ministry of Mike Crane, the founder of Karate for Christ International. During his ministry, Karate for Christ was a "traveling" ministry, using Martial Arts demonstrations to draw a crowd, and then preaching the gospel. Many people were saved as a result of this ministry.

Years later, another gentleman picked up where Karate for Christ International left off when Mike Crane's retired from traveling evangelism. At this time, Karate for Christ began to move into a more "school" based ministry. Joseph Lumpkin eventually became the President of Karate for Christ as we know it today. It was during his presidency that the ministry grew from a couple of schools in Alabama, to over 8,000 members world wide.

After the initial expansion of the ministry, Joseph Lumpkin retired the presidency to devote more time to Shinse Hapkido, a World Kido Federation recognized kwan of Hapkido. Daryl Covington then succeeded him as president. (Note: Shinsei can also be spelled "Shinse" in Korean. The spellings are used interchangeably.)

The ministry has now grown to over 20,000 members, and has seen over 424,000 people saved as a result of the gospel being presented. Due to the world wide nature of KFCI, the ministry has moved its headquarters to Seoul, South Korea, where the Covington family serves as missionaries.

The mission of KFCI is simple:

Our Mission:

To proclaim the Gospel of Jesus Christ. To reach the lost, mature the saints, serve our communities, and to touch the lives of "at risk youth" and families in need. To do these things throughout the world via the medium, lessons, and discipline of martial arts. To teach the best and most effective martial art we know. To serve God, minister to others, and teach the children well.

Statement of Faith:

We believe in the Trinity of God, the Virgin Birth, the inspired and preserved Word of God (Ps. 12:6-7), and It rightly divided (2 Tim. 2:15) that Jesus is God manifest in the flesh, and that He died on the Cross, was buried, and rose again on the third day, as according to Scripture, which was a witnessed event.. We are saved by grace through faith, not of works. Our calling is to equip the Christian Martial Artists to reach out to the lost. We refer theological and counseling issues back to the local church pastors, since our calling is to come alongside them, to win the lost, and to encourage believers to get into fellowship with a local church.

-

Dr. Daryl Covington

ABOUT KFCI SCHOOL / INSTRUCTOR CERTIFICATION

The Webster dictionary defines endorsement as approval. The Karate for Christ Certification process is all about receiving the KFCI stamp of approval. Why do we want you to become certified? We want you to become part of the team, because you can make a difference! KFCI ministries are reaching children, and adults for Jesus Christ. We want to officially validate your <u>Christian Ministry</u> as part of our team. Once you have successfully completed the process you will receive endorsement from Karate for Christ International.

INDEX / CONTENTS

Introduction

Chapter 1:   Standing Orders
Chapter 2:   Leadership, The Army Way
Chapter 3:   Teaching Martial Arts Philosophies and Traditions
Chapter 4:   Teaching the Way of the Hwa Rang Warrior
Chapter 5:   The Instructor's Creed
Chapter 6:   Tips to improve your Karate for Christ Ministry with Kids
Chapter 7:   A Pa Sa Ryu Philosophy of Teaching and Ministry (with Kang Rhee)
Chapter 8:   What Constitutes a Bible Ministry
Chapter 9:   The Way
Chapter 10:   What is an Instructor (by David Sheram)
Chapter 11:   Teaching the Sungja Do Way (by George Petrotta)
Chapter 12:   Getting the Actual Class Started
Chapter 13:   Karate for Christ Testimony (by David Dunn)
Chapter 14:   Teaching Special Needs Kids (by Char Englehardt)
Chapter 15:   Teaching Kids in General (by Chris Dewey)
Chapter 16:   Martial Arts and Christianity
Chapter 17:   Martial Arts and Meditation
Chapter 18:   Discipleship in Martial Arts
Chapter 19:   Christian Self Defense (with Don Englehardt)
Chapter 20:   False Teachers (with Donnie Bryson)
Chapter 21:   A Major Rule for all KFCI Members (by Joseph Lumpkin)
Chapter 22:   Karate for Christ International Black Belt Principles

Appendix A: Bible Study Starters for Class Devotions
                        Devotion 1
                        Devotion 2

Devotion 3
Devotion 4
Devotion 5
Devotion 6
Devotion 7
Devotion 8
Devotion 9
Devotion 10
Devotion 11
Devotion 12

Appendix B: The Martial Arts Library

Appendix C: The Bible Ministry Library

Appendix D: Contributed Essays

     1 The Importance of Integrity –
     by Michael Mason

     2 10 Ways to Raise a Street Smart Child –
     by Fariborz Ashakh

     3 Can a Christian Study Aikido –
     by Mark Barlow

     4 When Training Becomes Real Life –
     by Steve Riggs

     5 Get Up - by Joseph Lumpkin

Appendix E: Techniques and Tips to Keep Your Class from Getting Stale

Appendix F: Ministry Proposal Sample - by Steve Riggs

Appendix G: Karate for Christ Officers

Appendix H: Ranking Board and Guidelines (with Michael Lewis)

Appendix I: Certification Quiz

Appendix J: Asia Reach Support Documents

Appendix K: About Asia Reach Ministries

INTRODUCTION

For those that are interested in "certification" status with Karate for Christ International, you will find the full and complete guidelines for this process in Appendix H, in the back of this book. While all are welcome, and can join Karate for Christ International with out being "certified", our board thought it to be of the up most importance to "get to know" those that we will certify and can "officially" recommend.

CHAPTER 1:

STANDING ORDERS

As a former Paratrooper in the United States Army, I learned a great deal about standing orders. Those are orders you have that are always true. Perhaps the most famous set of "standing orders" are those of the U.S. Army Airborne Ranger.

The Rangers, originally "Roger's Rangers", were organized in 1756, by a gentleman from New Hampshire named Major Robert Rogers. Major Rogers recruited American colonists to aid the British during the French and Indian War. Using the techniques and methods of war characteristic of the Indians and frontiersmen in the colonies, Major Rogers incorporated this system into a "martial way", or way of fighting. These techniques were formally written in a document call *"Standing Orders"* in 1759.

These standing orders are nearly 250 years old, but they are still considered the "Standing Orders" of the U.S. Army Airborne Ranger, even today. This tells us that, standing orders, when well thought out, will stand the test of time. This book is designed to be a "standing orders" of such, for the way to do martial ministry. Not in detail, but an outline to stand the test of time.

Before we proceed, I would like the reader to consider those "standing orders" of the Rangers. They are still in the Ranger Handbook Today. Page *I* and *ii* of the Modern United State Army Ranger Handbook SH 21-76 have these orders, from 1759, listed as follows:

Don't forget nothing.

Have your musket clean as a whistle, hatchet scoured, sixty
    rounds power and ball, and be ready to march at a minute's
    warning.

When you're on the march, act the way you would if you was
    sneaking up on a deer. See the enemy first.

Tell the truth about what you see and what you do. There is an
    Army depending on us for correct information. You can lie all

you please when you tell other folks about the Rangers, but don't never lie to a Ranger or officer.

Don't never take a chance you don't have to.

When you're on the march we march single file, far enough apart so one shot can't go through two men.

If we strike swamps or soft ground, we spread out abreast, so it's hard to track us.

When we march, we keep moving till dark, so as to give the enemy the least possible chance at us.

When we camp, half the part stays awake while the other half sleeps.

If we take prisoners, we keep 'em separate till we have had time to examine them, so they can't cook up a story between 'em.

Don't ever march home the same way. Take a different route so you won't get ambushed.

No matter whether we travel in big parties or little ones, each party has to keep a scout twenty yards ahead, twenty yard on each flank and twenty yards in the rear, so the main body can't be surprised and wiped out.

Every night you'll be told where to meet if surrounded by a superior force.

Don't sit down to eat without posting sentries.

Don't sleep beyond dawn. Dawn's when the French and Indians attack.

Don't cross a river by a regular ford.

If somebody's trailing you, make a circle, come back onto your tracks, and ambush the folks that aim to ambush you.

Don't stand up when the enemy's coming against you. Kneel down, lie down, hide behind a tree.

Let the enemy come till he's almost close enough to touch. Then let him have it and jump out and finish him up with your hatchet.

Keep in remembrance, these orders were written at a time when men stood in straight lines and shot at each other. May this book serve the martial arts community in the way these orders have served their Rangers: Proven effective then, and now.

CHAPTER 2:

LEADERSHIP,

THE ARMY WAY

Perhaps an even greater way to look at the power and importance of leadership in the martial arts ministry setting is to look into the men that "Lead The Way". The U.S. Army Rangers. These Principles of Ranger Leadership will form the Outline for this book on "doing martial arts ministry" the right way.

Section 1-1 of the U.S. Army Ranger Handbook makes the following statements:

> The most essential element of combat power is competent and confident leadership. Leadership provides purpose, direction, and motivation in combat. It is the leader who will determine the degree to which maneuver, firepower, and protection are maximized; who will ensure these elements are effectively balanced; and who will decide how to bring them to bear against the enemy. While leadership requirements differ with unit size and type, all leaders must be men of character; they must know and understand soldiers and the material tools of war. They must act with courage and conviction in the uncertainty and confusion of battle. The primary function of tactical leaders is to induce soldiers to do difficult things in dangerous, stressful circumstances.

> As a leader, there are certain things that you must be, know, and do:

BE

COMMITTED TO THE PROFESSIONAL ARMY ETHIC
- loyalty to the nation's ideals
- loyalty to the unit
- selfless service
- personal responsibility

POSSESS PROFESSIONAL CHARACTER TRAITS
- Courage

- Commitment
- Candor
- Competence
- Integrity

KNOW

FOUR FACTORS OF LEADERSHIP AND HOW THEY AFFECT EACH OTHER
- Take Charge
- Communicate
- Motivate
- Supervise

KNOW YOURSELF
- Strengths and weaknesses of your character, knowledge, and skills

KNOW HUMAN NATURE
- Human needs and emotions
- How people respond to stress
- Strengths, weaknesses, knowledge and skills of your people

KNOW YOUR JOB
- Be technically and tactically proficient

KNOW YOUR UNIT
- How to develop necessary individual and team skills
- How to develop cohesion and discipline

DO

PROVIDE DIRECTION
- Goal Setting
- Problem Solving
- Decision Making
- Planning

IMPLEMENT
- Communicating
- Coordinating
- Supervising
- Evaluating

MOTIVATE
- Develop morale and esprit
- Teach
- Coach
- Counsel

CHAPTER 3:

TEACHING MARTIAL

ARTS PHILOSOPHIES

AND TRADITIONS

The martial arts not only art forms, they are specific fields of scientific study as well. In order to truly instruct, the Sensei must be both scientist and artist. Many students are taught forms and techniques, but if you are not teaching the traditions, theories, principles, laws and techniques upon which these techniques and forms are based, you are robbing the student of the artistry within the martial arts. It is after one is taught all these concepts that he is then able to practice them with passion and discipline, because he has caught a glimpse of understanding as to what and why he is doing, and what makes it work. It is then the student may begin to master the arts, and he himself becomes the artist.

CHAPTER 4:

TEACH THE WAY OF THE

HWA RANG WARRIOR

As a life long Korean martial arts practitioner, I have always been fascinated by the stories, myths, legends, and facts of the Hwa Rang Warriors. These warriors taught and lived by a warrior code and nine virtues. These are not only the basis for Korean Martial Arts, but have roots in Scripture as well.

Any Korean Martial Arts instructor should teach these to his students, and model them in life. By using the Code of the Ancient warrior, and the Scriptures listed, you can use a Traditional Warrior Code to teach Biblical principles to your students in a ministry setting.

A. The Hwa Rang Warrior Code

1. Be loyal to your country. (Romans 13:1-7)
Romans 13:1 Let every soul be subject unto the higher powers. For there is no power but of God: the powers that be are ordained of God.

13:2 Whosoever therefore resisteth the power, resisteth the ordinance of God: and they that resist shall receive to themselves damnation.

13:3 For rulers are not a terror to good works, but to the evil. Wilt thou then not be afraid of the power? Do that which is good, and thou shalt have praise of the same:

2. Be obedient to your parents. (Eph 6:1-3)
Ephesians 6:1 Children obey your parents in the Lord: for this is right.

6:2 Honor thy father and mother; which is the first commandment with promise;

6:3 That it may be well with thee, and thou mayest live long on the earth.

13:4 For he is the minister of God to thee for good. But if thou do that, which is evil, be afraid; for he beareth not the sword in vain: for he is the minister of God, a revenger to execute wrath upon him that doeth evil.

13:5 Wherefore ye must needs be subject, not only for wrath, but also for conscience sake.

13:6 For this cause pay ye tribute also: for they are God's ministers, attending continually upon this very thing.

13:7 Render therefore to all their dues: tribute to whom tribute is due; custom to whom custom; fear to whom fear; honor to whom honor.

3. Have faith and honor among friends. (Proverbs 17:17)
Proverbs 17:17 A friend loveth at all times, and a brother is born for adversity.

4. Perseverance in battle. (2 Samuel 23:8-12)
2 Samuel 23:8 These be the names of the mighty men whom David had: The Tachmonite that sat in the seat, chief among the captains; the same was Adino the Eznite: he lift up his spear against eight hundred, whom he slew at one time.

23:9 And after him was Eleazar the son of Dodo the Ahohite, one of the three mighty men with David, when they defied the Philistines that were there gathered together to battle, and the men of Israel were gone away:

23:10 He arose, and smote the Philistines until his hand was weary, and his hand clave unto the sword: and the LORD wrought a great victory that day; and the people returned after him only to spoil.

23:11 And after him was Shammah the son of Agee the Hararite. And the Philistines were gathered together into a troop, where was a piece of ground full of nowled: and the people fled from the Philistines.

23:12 But he stood in the midst of the ground, and defended it, and slew the Philistines: and the LORD wrought a great victory.

5. Justice (Ps 82:3)
82:3 Defend the poor and fatherless: do justice to the afflicted and needy.

B. The Hwa Rang Warriors Nine Lived Virtues

1.Hi – "humanity" (Job 12:9-10)
Job 12:9 Who knoweth not in all these that the hand of the LORD hath wrought this?

12:10 In whose hand is the soul of every living thing, and the breath of all mankind.

2. Sum – "goodness" (Ps. 33:4-5)
Psalm 33:4 For the word of the LORD is right; and all his works are done in truth.

33:5 He loveth righteousness and judgment: the earth is full of the goodness of the LORD.

3. Oui – "justice" (Micah 6:8)
Micah 6:8 He hath shewed thee, O man, what is good; and what doth the LORDrequire of thee, but to do justly, and to love mercy, and to walk humbly with thy God?

4. Duk – "virtue" (2Pe 1:5-8)
2 Peter 1:5 And beside this, giving all diligence, add to your faith virtue; and to virtue knowledge;

1:6 And to knowledge temperance; and to temperance patience; and to patience godliness;

1:7 And to godliness brotherly kindness; and to brotherly

kindness
charity.

1:8 For if these things be in you, and abound, they make you that ye shall neither be barren nor unfruitful in the knowledge of our Lord Jesus Christ.

5. Yeh – "courtesy" (Pr. 16:7)
Proverbs 16:7 When a man's ways please the LORD, he maketh even his enemies to be at peace with him.

6. Chung –"loyalty" (Pr. 17:17)
Proverbs 17:17 A friend loveth at all times, and a brother is born for adversity.

7. Ji – wisdom" (Ps. 111:10)
Psalm 111:10 The fear of the LORD is the beginning of wisdom: a good understanding have all they that do his commandments: his praise endureth for ever.

8. Yong – "courage" (Deut. 31:6)
Deuteronomy 31:6 Be strong and of a good courage, fear not, nor be afraid of them: for the LORD thy God, he it is that doth go with thee; he will not fail thee, nor forsake thee.

9. Sin – "trust" (Ps. 18:2)
Psalm 18:2 The LORD is my rock, and my fortress, and my deliverer; my God, my strength, in whom I will trust; my buckler, and the horn of my salvation, and my high tower.

Using these virtues and codes insures the student understands the purpose behind the martial arts training he is receiving, learns about the Korean culture, and is exposed to Biblical truth.

CHAPTER 5:

THE INSTRUCTOR'S

CREED

To be a "certified" instructor with Karate for Christ International, one must take this creed to heart, and apply these Biblical principles within the confines of his class.

1. I will teach this class as if it is the most important class I'll ever teach.

> *Exodus 18:20 And thou shalt teach them ordinances and laws, and shalt shew them the way wherein they must walk, and the work that they must do.*

2. I am patient and enthusiastic.

> *Luke 8:15 But that on the good ground are they, which in an honest and good heart, having heard the word, keep it, and bring forth fruit with patience.*

3. I am cheerful! No matter how bad I feel before putting on my uniform, the moment I cinch the knot in my belt, my attitude must change.

> *Proverbs 15:13 A merry heart maketh a cheerful countenance: but by sorrow of the heart the spirit is broken.*

4. I am consistent! Steady attendance is a must. The instructors and students are counting on me.

> *1Timothy 5:17 Let the elders that rule well be counted worthy of double honour, especially they who labour in the word and doctrine.*

5. I am never unconstructively critical! Instead I am constructively helpful.

> *Matthew 12:36 But I say unto you, That every idle word that men shall speak, they shall give account thereof in the day of judgment.*

6. I am a good talent finder! I see the good in my students and I tell them about it.

> *Eph 4:29 Let no corrupt communication proceed out of your mouth, but that which is good to the use of edifying, that it may minister grace unto the hearers.*
> *1Thesalonians 5:11 Wherefore comfort yourselves together, and edify one another, even as also ye do.*

7. I never punish, I discipline! Discipline is done out of love, punishment is done out of anger.

> *Deuteronomy 8:5 Thou shalt also consider in thine heart, that, as a man chasteneth his son, so the LORD thy God chasteneth thee.*

> *Proverbs 13:24 He that spareth his rod hateth his son: but he that loveth him chasteneth him betimes.*

> *Hebrews 12:6 For whom the Lord loveth he chasteneth, and scourgeth every son whom he receiveth.*

> *12:7 If ye endure chastening, God dealeth with you as with sons; for what son is he whom the father chasteneth not?*

8. I understand the importance of touch (appropriate touch), eye contact, and calling students by their names.

> *Colossians 2:2 That their hearts might be comforted, being knit together in love, and unto all riches of the full assurance of understanding, to the acknowledgment of the mystery of God, and of the Father, and of Christ;*

9. I go the extra mile, always giving more than the expected amount.

Matthew 5:41 And whosoever shall compel thee to go a mile, go with him twain.

10. I treat every student I meet like they are the most important people. Why?

(a) Because they are important.

(b) We should treat all people with respect. They will give us their friendship and respect in return.

Acts 10:34 Then Peter opened his mouth, and said, Of a truth I perceive that God is no respecter of persons:

10:35 But in every nation he that feareth him, and worketh righteousness, is accepted with him.

10:36 The word which God sent unto the children of Israel, preaching peace by Jesus Christ: (he is Lord of all☺

11. I will lead by example.

John 13:15 For I have given you an example, that ye should do as I have done to you.

CHAPTER 6:

TIPS TO

IMPROVE YOUR KARATE

FOR CHRIST MINISTRY

WITH KIDS

There is a huge difference in a Christian martial arts program and a martial arts ministry. If you are a Christian and teach martial arts, you may have a "Christian" martial arts program, but that does not constitute a ministry. The program becomes a ministry when you realize the greatest thing the kids will learn is the Bible.

Psalm 119:105 Thy word is a lamp unto my feet, and a light unto my path.

Most Christian martial arts programs never turn into ministry because of the lackadaisical way the instructor approaches the "devotion", or "Bible study". In order for your class to be a ministry, the Bible cannot be a "tack on", it must take the prominent place in all that you do. It is the *hyung*, the pattern, the *kata*, the form, by which all must be taught. With this in mind, let us now look to some important aspects on improving our martial arts ministry.

1. Prepare All Week

I have witnessed time and time again well-meaning instructors "toss" a Scripture or two together and say it was a Bible study. We must realize we are called to be stewards of the Word of God (1 Corinthians 4:1), and must wield that Sword (Ephesians 6:17) with great accuracy, practice, and preparation.

1Corinthians 4:1 Let a man so account of us, as of the ministers of Christ, and stewards of the mysteries of God

Ephesians 6:17 And take the helmet of salvation, and the sword of the Spirit, which is the word of God:

Be honest. How may times have you picked up the Bible on the way into your "martial arts ministry" class, and just "flung something out there", as we would say in South Mississippi. That is not fair to your kids, and it is not doing justice to the perfect Word of God. Do something ever day to get ready for the Bible study portion of your class. Remember that you can teach all the self-defense in the world, and none of it will do any good against the flames of Hell.

Matthew 10:28 And fear not them which kill the body, but are not able to kill the soul: but rather fear him which is able to destroy both soul and body in hell.

2. Prepare yourself first

When I first started preaching, I used to think ministry was about preparing a message and delivering that message. Now, I know that is wrong. Ministry is about preparing the preacher, and delivering the preacher. What do I mean by this? Never neglect your personal spiritual preparation or time with the Lord Jesus Christ. You must spend time with the Lord and His Word if you care going to teach it to kids, or anyone for that matter.

Ex 15:2 The LORD is my strength and song, and he is become my salvation: he is my God, and I will prepare him an habitation; my father's God, and I will exalt him.

15:3 The LORD is a man of war: the LORD is his name.

3. Beware of Easy Fixes

Sometimes you may not have the time to do all the preparing you want, but I encourage you to stay away from the "easy, canned devotion". Reading a cute story is not true ministry. If you do not have time to prepare, at least give the kids some Bible verse drills.

2Timothy 2:15 Study to shew thyself approved unto God, a workman that needeth not to be ashamed, rightly dividing the word of truth.

The Word must do this thing, not we poor sinners – Martin Luther, Reformer

4. Deal with Disciple up front

If the kids misbehave, deal with it appropriately, especially during Bible time. When kids know the boundaries, they stay inside them for the most part. Make sure you establish them well.

Job 36:9 Then he sheweth them their work, and their transgressions that they have exceeded.

36:10 He openeth also their ear to discipline, and commandeth that they return from iniquity.

36:11 If they obey and serve him, they shall spend their days in prosperity, and their years in pleasures.

5. Know what the kids think about your class.

Are they looking forward to it? Are they bored? What are they telling their friends? Are they growing in the Lord? In short: Keep score.

Proverbs 22:6 Train up a child in the way he should go: and when he is old, he will not depart from it.

6. Personal Discipline

A lack of preparation, both physically and spiritually, will be perceived by the kids and parents. If you do not pray and prepare, the ministry will suffer.

Luke 18:1 And he spake a parable unto them to this end, that men ought always to pray, and not to faint;

7. Is this Important?

In the Shinse System, we take great pride in the fact that we "trim away the fat", meaning we focus on the techniques that are important and needed. This is needed in your ministry as well. Telling stories about Jonah and the Great Fish may be entertaining, but are your kids learning practical application? Are they realizing the Bible is more than a storybook? Make sure that you don't just "tell the story", but rather, you "tell why the story is important". Watch your life, and your doctrine. Teach doctrine, and make it apply to life. By doing these things, you will see results in your ministry.

Timothy 4:11 These things command and teach.

4:12 Let no man despise thy youth; but be thou an example of the believers, in word, in conversation, in charity, in spirit, in faith, in purity.

4:13 Till I come, give attendance to reading, to exhortation, to doctrine.

4:14 Neglect not the gift that is in thee, which was given thee by prophecy, with the laying on of the hands of the presbytery.

4:15 Meditate upon these things; give thyself wholly to them; that thy profiting may appear to all.

4:16 Take heed unto thyself, and unto the doctrine; continue in them: for in doing this thou shalt both save thyself, and them that hear thee.

8. Mentor others

If you are the instructor, began to teach others how to teach the Bible to kids. Do not just say, "YOU, bring the devotion next week". Mentor your students in more than the arts. Teach them to fight the good spiritual battle.

Ephesians 6:12 For we wrestle not against flesh and blood, but against principalities, against powers, against the rulers of the darkness of this world, against spiritual wickedness in high places.

CHAPTER 7:

A PA SA RYU

PHILOSOPHY OF

TEACHING AND

MINISTRY

By Kang Rhee, as interviewed by Daryl Covington

(Scriptures and words in parenthesis added by the Daryl Covington)

Perhaps one of the greatest philosophical influences in my life (Covington) has been Master Kang Rhee. A few days prior to writing this portion of the book, I sat in his office anxiously as he wrote in *Hangul* (Korean script) on my newly obtained 4th Dan certificate. His leadership and teaching skills have been greatly influential in my life, but we will spend this chapter peering into the unique methodology that makes Kang Rhee a true master of ministry.

The Interview begins:

"Dr. Eagle", he said. "It is a long journey from here to Washington D.C. There are many rest areas for one to stop and rest, all the while being on the journey. Your life is long to go, you need to slow down. Don't drive from here to Washington without stopping at each area". Those were words I needed to hear. For months I had been on the go: getting Shinse recognized, pastoring a church, being President of Karate for Christ International, and the list goes on. I had indeed been "Driving" without "Stopping to rest".

> *Matthew 11:28 Come unto me, all ye that labour and are heavy laden, and I will give you rest.*

The conversation continued, "The head of this system (Shinse) can be the King of the Jungle, or the King of the Desert. The King of the Jungle has the respect of all the animals, and lives in harmony. The king of the Desert defeats and destroys, and then rules a wasteland alone".

These things I continually contemplate as I write Master Rhee's philosophies of the arts and of life. His biography is immense. Kang Rhee was the Instructor of Elvis Presley and Bill "Superfoot" Wallace. He Graduated (B.A. Business) from Yonsei University in Seoul, Korea, and established and served as Captain of Yonsei University Martial Arts Team. (Life is very surprising. As I write, I now attend advanced language classes at Yonsei University in Seoul!). He was the head instructor of the Korean Military Intelligence Group's Officers.

Kang Rhee has trained in *Kong Soo Do, Chang Mu Kwan, Kwon Bup, Kang Duk Won,* and *Han Kuk Hap Ki Do*. It is from this extensive background that he Established *Pa Sa Ryu Mu Do* Association in Memphis, Tennessee, in 1966. In 1975 he was granted the *Seventh Dan Kuk Ki Won* (Headquarters of *Tae Kwon Do* in Seoul, Korea) 1975. He now holds an 9th from that organization, and is the founder of the *Pa Sa Ryu Tae Kwon Do* System.

He is the producer of Annual Charity Karate Championship Fund Raiser for St. Jude Children's Research Hospital in Memphis, and has received the State of Tennessee Governor's Award, the City of Memphis Mayor Certificate of Appreciation for Various Community Services in 1982, 1989, and 1999, and has been a Member of President of the United States's Advisory Council on Democratic and Peaceful Unification of Republic of Korea since 1991. He currently teaches at the Kang Rhee Institute, in Cordova, Tennessee.

The interview continues:

Principles

Through Pa Sa Ryu, Master Rhee teaches the constant improvement and refinement of technique, and the development of the total person. "A Christian Martial Artist should be the best person in the world", he stated. "He is refining the body through Martial Arts, and having his soul refined by the Holy Spirit". Pa Sa Ryu is a contemporary martial art style combining both traditional and modern applications. It teaches logical techniques. "It is my belief that by teaching Martial Arts, I can guide my students to the realization of their fullest potential", Master Rhee states.

Ephesians 6:10 Finally, my brethren, be strong in the Lord, and in the power of his might.

Kang Rhee on Training for Adults

While the ability to defend against a physical attack is important, defense against stress and its effects is of greater importance. Kang Rhee desires the adult to become a master person. Training in the martial arts is an excellent means of stress management because it challenges and expands the mind while providing a heart-strengthening workout, all in an enthusiastic and exciting environment. Kang Rhee incorporates *Karate, Tae Kwon Do* and *Kung Fu* to create *Pa Sa Ryu* which is appropriate for all body styles and structures. The physical workout strengthens and elongates the musculature as coordination enhances manual dexterity. Opening the body to new experiences improves attitude, increases concentration skills, and develops leadership ability.

> *1Corinthians 9:25 And every man that striveth for the mastery is temperate in all things. Now they do it to obtain a corruptible crown; but we an incorruptible.*
>
> *9:26 I therefore so run, not as uncertainly; so fight I, not as one that beateth the air:*
>
> *9:27 But I keep under my body, and bring it into subjection: lest that by any means, when I have preached to others, I myself should be a castaway.*

Kang Rhee Training for Children

The most important thing for parents to consider when choosing a martial arts school is to understand that a child's martial arts instructor can be one of the most influential people in a child's life. Parents should choose an instructor who will reinforce the values that are being taught in the home and set a good, stable example for the child. The quality of the instructor is much more important than the style of martial arts practiced. While parents understand the obvious benefits of their children being able to defend themselves, many assume that strict discipline will be enforced in the classes and that by being in a disciplined environment, children will learn to be more disciplined outside the martial art. Kang Rhee employs a different theory. He stresses true self-discipline rather than imposed discipline, which necessitates a more patient approach.

Several "tools" are used to accomplish this goal including positive motivation. Positive motivation (praising/rewarding good behavior while avoiding criticism whenever possible) builds true confidence without arrogance. This confidence affords the child the courage to try something new/different without fear of failure. Kang Rhee also employs the use of setting short and long-term goals, demonstrating to the child that a goal can be accomplished with hard work, determination, and proper planning.

Kang Rhee uses the child's fascination with the martial arts techniques to capture the child's attention and expand the child's attention span. An expanded attention span allows the child to learn to focus his/her mental energy, thus absorbing and retaining more knowledge. This ability to focus naturally results in self-discipline and ultimately translates into other areas such as schoolwork.

Parents often question the value of sparring. Kang Rhee explains that "sparring is a useful tool teaching timing, balance, application and dexterity; however, it is most valuable as a controlled opportunity for an individual to learn to recognize and control the effects of adrenaline, which is one of the most powerful endocrine substances created within the human body. The ability to control adrenaline-generated responses is paramount to self-control and self-discipline". No child should ever be forced to spar; however, when interest is expressed it should be encouraged. For safety, he requires all participants must wear proper protective equipment.

The Pa SaRyu Philosophy

The following is taken by permission from Master Kang Rhee from the Pa Sa Ryu Instructor's Handbook:

A *Pa Sa Ryu* Martial Artist is a person who is developing certain characteristics, which make him special and unique. He is stable and dependable. He realizes that he has responsibilities and duties in all areas of his life and that these must be fulfilled before he can be a true *Pa Sa Ryu* Martial Artist. He is committed to the philosophy of *SUN* and all that it means. When he comes to training class, he gives his best efforts and is consistent in his training. He realizes the importance of regular training, and he organizes his time so that regular class sessions are a part of his life.

A *Pa Sa Ryu* Martial Artist has enthusiasm for his art and for life. He realizes that without enthusiasm, life is dull and commonplace. He also realizes that he controls his attitudes and he makes the effort to cultivate the attitude of enthusiasm. A true *Pa Sa Ryu* Martial Artist glows with the sunshine of optimism. People are drawn to him because he makes people happy by his positive approach to life.

He knows that no matter what his rank, whether White or Black belt, he never stops learning. He never reaches the goal of perfection but he must keep striving toward that goal. A *Pa Sa Ryu* Martial Artist knows that he has an obligation to pass on his knowledge of techniques and the philosophy of *SUN* to others who are striving to learn while he learns from them. He is aware that he has arrived at his level because someone cared enough to take their time and energies to help him.

2Pe 3:18 But grow in grace, and in the knowledge of our Lord and Saviour Jesus Christ. To him be glory both now and for ever. Amen.

SUN is a unique expression used by *Pa Sa Ryu* Martial Artist Association members to show respect. It Came from *Chung Doe Sun Hang*, whose philosophy is that each martial artist is an _expression of self-respect, self-discipline, ambition, and appreciation. "*SUN* makes evil Shadows disappear".

Psalm 84:11 For the LORD God is a sun and shield: the LORD will give grace and glory: no good thing will he withhold from them that walk uprightly.

The *Pa Sa Ryu* Martial Artist is straight-forward and honest, without arrogance or hypocrisy. He is proud and confident, but gentle, knowing that "Nothing is so strong as gentleness, nothing so gentle as real strength".

The true *Pa Sa Ryu* martial Artist knows that he must have long-term goals for his life. He lives today fully, but he also looks ahead and plots his future course as a ship's captain lays out his plans for a sea voyage. This person has a plan, which consists of systematic, step-by-step approach to his major goal in life. He is sharp and balances as he accomplishes one goal after another toward his ultimate life-long goal – the contribution to this world, which he alone can make. He devotes himself to that goal.

> *Matthew 6:19 Lay not up for yourselves treasures upon earth, where moth and rust doth corrupt, and where thieves break through and steal:*
>
> *6:20 But lay up for yourselves treasures in heaven, where neither moth nor rust doth corrupt, and where thieves do not break through nor steal:*
>
> *6:21 For where your treasure is, there will your heart be also.*

The *Pa Sa Ryu* Martial Artist has a realistic approach to life. He knows that by "trying to chase too many rabbits" he loses his focus and his efforts are in vain. He is self-controlled. He directs his life toward the area, which gives him the most satisfaction and offers opportunity to contribute to society. He has a professional attitude and he approaches every challenge with the determination to be the best that he can be.

Philippians 4:13 I can do all things through Christ which strengtheneth me.

A *Pa Sa Ryu* Martial Artist is young, old, middle-aged – a woman, a man, or a child. He or she may be tall or short, with physical strength, or physically weak. He may be talented or slow learning – but whatever traits the person has, he is accepted and welcomed by his fellow members. He is expected only to give his best efforts and maintain a good attitude. He competes with no one, only himself. He is expected to know that, "There is no failure except in giving up.

> *Ephesians 6:18 Praying always with all prayer and supplication in the Spirit, and watching there unto with all perseverance and supplication for all saints;*

The worst bankrupt is the world is the man who has lost his enthusiasm. Let him lose everything but enthusiasm and he will come through again to success. No life ever grows great until it is focused, dedicated, disciplined."

CHAPTER 8:

WHAT CONSTITUTES A

BIBLE MINISTRY

Teaching martial arts in a church building does not make the class a ministry. Being a Christian and a martial arts teacher does not make what you are doing a ministry. Martin Luther said, "The Word must do this thing, not we poor sinners". In order to have a "ministry", to minister to the students in the biblical sense, one must minister the Word of God.

Ps 18:30 As for God, his way is perfect: the word of the LORD is tried: he is a buckler to all those that trust in him.

Pr 30:5 Every word of God is pure: he is a shield unto them that put their trust in him

Mt 4:4 But he answered and said, It is written, Man shall not live by bread alone, but by every word that proceedeth out of the mouth of God.

Lu 4:4 And Jesus answered him, saying, It is written, That man shall not live by bread alone, but by every word of God.

Lu 11:28 But he said, Yea rather, blessed are they that hear the word of God, and keep it.

Ro 10:17 So then faith cometh by hearing, and hearing by the word of God.

Eph 6:17 And take the helmet of salvation, and the sword of the Spirit, which is the word of God

1Th 2:13 For this cause also thank we God without ceasing, because, when ye received the word of God which ye heard of us, ye received it not as the word of men, but as it is in truth, the word of God, which effectually worketh also in you that believe.

2Ti 2:9 Wherein I suffer trouble, as an evil doer, even unto bonds; but the word of God is not bound.

2Ti 2:15 Study to shew thyself approved unto God, a workman that needeth not to be ashamed, rightly dividing the word of truth.

Tit 1:3 But hath in due times manifested his word through preaching, which is committed unto me according to the commandment of God our Saviour;

Heb 4:12 For the word of God is quick, and powerful, and sharper than any two-edged sword, piercing even to the dividing asunder of soul and spirit, and of the joints and marrow, and is a discerner of the thoughts and intents of the heart.

Ps 12:6 The words of the LORD are pure words: as silver tried in a furnace of earth, purified seven times. 7 Thou shalt keep them, O LORD, thou shalt preserve them from this generation for ever.

God has purified His Word, kept It, and preserved It. If you do not use the Bible, you have NO MINISTRY!

CHAPTER 9:

THE WAY

As martial artists, we are always talking about "the way", or "DO" (pronounced D-O-E). This is a generic term used to describe the journey one enters when he begins the life long study of martial arts. The way of *Shinse Hapkido* is a great way, a great journey, but there is a far more important road to travel. That is the Roman Road.

The "Roman Road" is named after the sixth book in the New Testament. Paul the Apostle, wrote a letter to the Christians in Rome. His letter is thus known as ROMANS. Paul wrote some specific things necessary to believe in order to be saved. "Being saved" means: When we repent, God forgives all our sins and sinful nature. What are we saved from? He (God/Jesus) SAVES us:

- From the nature of sin we were born with; To a new nature born of His Spirit.

– From the control of sin; To the loving control of God.

– From the Penalty of sin; To the reward of the righteousness in JESUS. Being saved is being "born again." We are saved to a new life.

The Roman Road is a collection of verses in Paul's Epistle to the Romans that offers a clear and structured path to Jesus Christ. Although many people believe they will go to heaven because they have lived a good life, done charity work, been baptized as a child, attended church, or treated others fairly, the Bible declares that none of us can live up to God's standards of righteousness. Therefore, we need a road to God that doesn't rely on anything we do, but rather, relies on the gift of His grace alone.

Here is a simple map to help you follow the Roman Way, or Road:

The Roman Road provides a detailed map for our salvation and eternal fellowship with God. Just follow these steps:

We must acknowledge God as the Creator of everything,

accepting our humble position in God's created order and purpose.

Romans 1:19 Because that which may be known of God is manifest in them; for God hath shewed it unto them.

1:20 For the invisible things of him from the creation of the world are clearly seen, being understood by the things that are made, even his eternal power and Godhead; so that they are without excuse:

1:21 Because that, when they knew God, they glorified him not as God, neither were thankful; but became vain in their imaginations, and their foolish heart was darkened.

2. We must realize that we are sinners and that we need forgiveness. None of us are worthy under God's standards.

Romans 3:23, For all have sinned, and come short of the glory of God.

3. God gave us the way to be forgiven of our sins. He showed us His love by giving us the potential for life through the death of His Son, Jesus Christ.

Romans 5:8 But God commendeth his love toward us, in that, while we were yet sinners, Christ died for us.

4. If we remain sinners, we will die. However, if we repent of our sins, and accept Jesus Christ as our Lord and Savior, we will have eternal life.

Romans 6:23 For the wages of sin is death; but the gift of God is eternal life through Jesus Christ our Lord.

5. Confess that Jesus Christ is Lord and believe in your heart that God raised Him from the dead and you are saved.

Romans 10:9 That if thou shalt confess with thy mouth the Lord Jesus, and shalt believe in thine heart that God hath raised him from the dead, thou shalt be saved.

10:10 For with the heart man believeth unto righteousness; and with the mouth confession is made unto salvation.

10:11 For the scripture saith, Whosoever believeth on him shall not be ashamed.

6. There are no other religious formulas or rituals. Just call upon the name of the Lord and you will be saved!

Romans 10:13 For whosoever shall call upon the name of the Lord shall be saved.

7. Determine in your heart to make Jesus Christ the Lord of your life today.

Romans 11:36 For of him, and through him, and to him, are all things: to whom be glory for ever. Amen.

8. So how do you go about that? Here is the pattern, the kata, the hyung, as found in God's Word:

Romans 3:23 For all have sinned, and come short of the glory of God

Romans 6:23 For the wages of sin is death; but the gift of God is eternal life through Jesus Christ our Lord.

Romans 5:8 But God commendeth his love toward us, in that, while we were yet sinners, Christ died for us.

Romans 10:9 That if thou shalt confess with thy mouth the Lord Jesus, and shalt believe in thine heart that God hath raised him from the dead, thou shalt be saved.

God tells us in the Bible how we can come to Him by being saved through Jesus Christ His Son. The proceeding salvation plan lays out the way you can know you will have eternal life in Jesus and have a lasting relationship with the Father. Then you are truly on the right "WAY".

CHAPTER 10:

WHAT IS AN

INSTRUCTOR?

In order to be a good teacher, instructor, *Sa Bum Nim,* or *Sensei,* we must understand what it means to be this person of influence. The following Chapter is contributed by David Sheram to help the Karate for Christ International Instructor understand what it truly means to be an "Instructor":

Our goal in teaching is to be like the Master Teacher, Jesus Christ. A quality teacher must be Christ-like. The best training comes from modeling.

> **Matthew 5:16 Let your light so shine before men, that they may see your good works, and glorify your Father which is in heaven.**

Our students will become like us. How we stand, they will stand. How we punch, they will punch. How we move, they will move. How we act, they will act. How we exemplify Jesus in our families, dojangs, business ethics, and personal lives, they will want to be the same way. We should deliver what we believe to be the truth.

Formal training is important but we need not only be martial arts instructors but we need to ensure that we are: born again, love people, prepared and apt to teach, always ready to learn, grounded in the Word, empowered with prayer and filled with the Spirit. In Ephesians 6:14 the Apostle Paul told the church in Ephesus to, ***"Stand therefore, having your loins girt about with truth"***. A quality instructor, the real Black Belt, must always wear the belt of truth. Honesty with students shows integrity. Our integrity is what we are even when no one else is around. We should be blameless, above reproach.

The mark of an excellent teacher is not so much the ability to impart information, but a contagious enthusiasm for learning.

In teaching, there are several points to remember:

> Instructing is a challenge for you to use all of your knowledge, skill, and patience.

Beginners are very fragile. The first three classes are the most important.

Practice the K.I.S.S. Principle. (Keep It Short and Simple).

Every student is different. Have patience.

Use the student's name often. Be personable.

Discouragement and lack of confidence are the enemies of the student.

Change the class structure from time to time. Keep it interesting.

Maintain discipline at all times.

Know the rules and follow them, but remember, "Knowledge is knowing the rules. Experience is knowing the exceptions to the rules."

Any student who desires extra help should get it. It could come from you or an Assistant Instructor.

Remind the students of the rules often.

Take your time. Do it right. We are not in a race.

Don't look for perfection at first.

Pick out the main problem and correct it.

Always demonstrate in the same direction as the student.

At times, you must have a commanding voice.

Speak clearly and loud enough for the student to understand.

Keep the student active.

Use a variety of techniques.

Keep the class interesting and not boring.

Plan the workouts. Be organized.

Encourage and compliment them often.

Introduce them to other students.

Do not expect too much too soon.

Do not let them feel dumb, uncoordinated, or that they are not progressing.

The Instructor

Throughout the past thirty-six years in the martial arts, I have taught approximately twenty-five instructor's courses. Following is an acrostic I use. I pray it will be of service.

I- Inventive
N- (K)nowledgeable
S- Studious
T- Teachable
R- Reliable
U- Understanding
C- Creative
T- Tenacious
O- Organized
R- Responsible

I-Inventive: A quality instructor is quick to think. There is always a way to explain how, when a student does not understand. Each student's body is different. Help the student to adapt. There could be physically or mentally challenged students that need fresh and or simple ways to learn. If they do not exist, invent them. Find a way!

N-(K) nowledgeable: A quality instructor knows what he is talking about. Do not try to "pull the wool over their eyes" or fake it. If you do not know find out. Tell them you don't know. Not only does an instructor know about his own art, he also knows about many others. Many questions will be asked. Find the answers. Your students depend on you.

> *Hosea 4:6 My people are destroyed for lack of knowledge: because thou hast rejected knowledge, I will also reject thee, that thou shalt be no priest to me: seeing thou hast forgotten the law of thy God, I will also forget thy children.*

S-Studious: Study! Practice! "Practice does not make perfect. Practice makes permanent. Proper practice makes perfect." Read! Read all you can about your art and others. If you have questions, ask your instructor. The answer can be found. Search for it!

> *Jeremiah 29:13 And ye shall seek me, and find me, when ye shall search for me with all your heart.*

T-Teachable: An instructor never stops learning. The "know it all" syndrome comes from pride. Pride was the first sin. It is still a sin. No one person knows it all. Be teachable. In other words, be able to be taught. Allow your instructors to teach you. Do not be arrogant. Humble yourself. We bow to one another in class. Therefore, learn a Scripture:

> *Luke 14:11 For whosoever exalteth himself shall be abased; and he that humbleth himself shall be exalted.*

As any quality instructor knows, our students help teach us about becoming better teachers. Their demands, problems, questions, and hunger for knowledge challenge us to be teachable. Learn also from your students. They will help you learn better teaching methods.

3:18 But grow in grace, and in the knowledge of our Lord and Saviour Jesus Christ. To him be glory both now and for ever. Amen.

R-Reliable: An instructor is on time. An instructor should never be late for class or come unprepared unless a grave emergency has transpired. Even then, someone is notified. A student, regardless of rank, should be able to depend on his instructor. Be there for them. Their lives are more than the Dojang. Not only are you Dojang reliable, you are personally reliable. They can count on you for support, encouragement, counseling, and prayer.

U-Understanding: Students have problems just as you have problems. Be understanding of life's situations but help instill responsibility. Be a listener. Sometimes students just need to vent. Be a counselor. Give Godly and Biblically sound advice. Know the Word of God and convey it in word and deed.

John 8:32 And ye shall know the truth, and the truth shall make you free.

C-Creative: Creativity goes beyond being inventive. Think of new ways to teach a simple technique. Plan ahead of time. Use analogies and parables in your teaching.

Matthew 13:3 And he spake many things unto them in parables, saying, Behold, a sower went forth to sow;

13:4 And when he sowed, some seeds fell by the way side, and the fowls came and devoured them up:

13:5 Some fell upon stony places, where they had not much earth: and forthwith they sprung up, because they had no deepness of earth:

13:6 And when the sun was up, they were scorched; and because they had no root, they withered away.

13:7 And some fell among thorns; and the thorns sprung up , and choke them:

13:8 But other fell into good ground, and brought forth fruit, some an hundredfold, some sixtyfold, some thirtyfold.

13:9 Who hath ears to hear, let him hear.

Use personal experiences. Students also want to know about you. God is a creator; that is far more than being an inventor. Your words can create excitement or discouragement. Your words can build up or tear down. Your words can create a learning environment or destroy one. Be creative. Speak life and learning into their lives.

T-Tenacious: Be persistent. Hold firm to what you know is right. Do not give up on your students. Do not let them go. Teach them the right way and the best way.

Ephesians 6:13 Wherefore take unto you the whole armour of God, that ye may be able to withstand in the evil day, and having done all, to stand.

God has not given up on you; don't give up on them.

O-Organized: Have a plan. Someone once said, "If you fail to plan, you plan to fail." Know what you are going to do for that class. Don't just "shoot from the hip". You will miss the target more often than hit the bull's eye. Plan a Saturday class in a park. Take the mats out there. They can be washed. Plan for another special instructor to come and teach specific techniques; such as, kicks breakfalls, wrist techniques, throws, etc. Advertise. They won't come if they don't know about it.

R-Responsible: You are responsible for the material you place into the lives of your students. You will be held responsible. Don't lead them astray.

18:6 But whoso shall offend one of these little ones which believe in me, it were better for him that a millstone were hanged about his neck, and that he were drowned in the depth of the sea.

18:7 Woe unto the world because of offences! For it must needs be that offences come; but woe to that man by whom the offence cometh!

18:8 Wherefore if thy hand or thy foot offend thee, cut them off, and cast them from thee: it is better for thee to enter into life halt or maimed, rather than having two hands or two feet to be cast into everlasting fire.

18:9 And if thine eye offend thee, pluck it out, and cast it from thee: it is better for thee to enter into life with one eye, rather than having two eyes to be cast into hell fire.

18:10 Take heed that ye despise not one of these little ones; for I say unto you, That in heaven their angels do always behold the face of my Father which is in heaven.

18:11 For the Son of man is come to save that which was lost.

Whatever the age, the beginners are always the "little ones". They depend on you to show them the way. Are we to show them only our way or The Way? The pure, holy, and righteous way. *Shinse* is "The Holy and True Martial Way". Teach them, show them, live it before them. Be more than an instructor; be a mentor. Disciple them.

Matthew 28:18 And Jesus came and spake unto them, saying, All power is given unto me in heaven and in earth.

28:19 Go ye therefore, and teach all nations, baptizing them in the name of the Father, and of the Son, and of the Holy Ghost:

28:20 Teaching them to observe all things whatsoever I have commanded you: and, lo, I am with you I, even unto the end of the world. Amen.

CHAPTER 11:

TEACHING THE SUNGJA

DO WAY

This chapter of the book is contributed by Dr. George Petrotta, head of the Korean systems promotions for Karate for Christ International. He offers some things that the martial arts ministry leader must teach. (Note: Dr. Daryl R. Covington, President of Karate for Christ International, also serves as the Director for George Petrotta's International Sungja Do Association in Korea).

(Scriptures and words in parenthesis added by the author of this book).

1. Teach the *Taekwondo* Student Oath
I shall obey the Tenets of *Taekwondo*.
I shall obey my Instructor and senior students.
I shall never misuse *Taekwondo*.
I will be a champion of freedom and injustice.
I will help build a more peaceful world.

2. Teaching Martial Arts Rituals and Traditions
Over the years, the martial arts have developed traditions of their own; as well as picking up those of the cultures in which they were developed. There are many martial arts from several countries and each art has many styles. We practice the *Chang-Hun* and Olympic style of *Taekwondo* as well as the *Tae-Pung Kwan* of *Hosin-do* and *Sungjado Tae Kwon Do*. Our rituals and traditions come from Korea but many of them are practiced in most martial arts.

a. Bowing:
Bowing is often misunderstood by people outside of the martial arts. In the Orient, bowing is a sign of respectful greeting – not a sign of submission or worship. To bow to another person is to indicate that you trust him enough to willingly take your eyes off of him. In the West, we shake hands. This grew out of the battlefield practice of clasping the enemy's sword-drawing hand during negotiations to insure that he could not draw his sword. Today it is used as a greeting. In the Bible, there was another way

of greeting:

Romans 16:16 Salute one another with an holy kiss. The churches of Christ salute you.

Bowing to instructors and fellow students is a sign of respectful greeting. Bowing to the United States flag shows respect for the nation we live in. Bowing to the flags of other countries shows respect for the country where our martial arts originated. There is no worship involved only respect.

b. Uniforms:

The first martial arts uniforms were nothing more than the common street clothes of the people of China, Korea, Okinawa and Japan. In the late 1800's, Dr. Jigaro Kano invented the sport of Judo and invented a reinforced Jacket for Judoka to wear so the students' throwing techniques would not tear their clothes off. This uniform became modified over the years until we have our current uniforms.

Ephesians 6:11 Put on the whole armour of God, that ye may be able to stand against the wiles of the devil.

c. Belts:

Many people, including martial artists, are confused about belts and their colors. For many centuries, the belt did not signify rank. Again, it was Dr. Kano, the founder of Judo, who introduced the use of different belt colors to denote ranks. He did this to make it easy to identify different ranks for competition. Different systems use different colors. Most Chinese martial arts don't use belts but use sashes instead. In Japanese martial arts, the belt was used to keep the jacket closed and was white. With years of practice, the belt would become soiled and stained and would eventually turn black. The colors used in the Korean martial arts are based on the colored robes worn by the different classes of royalty in the ancient Kingdom of Silla.

1Corinthians 9:24 Know ye not that they which run in a race run all, but one receiveth the prize? So run, that ye may obtain.

9:25 And every man that striveth for the mastery is temperate in all things. Now they do it to obtain a corruptible crown; but we an incorruptible.

d. Rank Promotion:

After two to three months, you should be ready for your first rank promotion. What does it mean to go up in rank? Does it mean that you have perfected a certain amount of knowledge? No. Rank promotion means that you have an adequate grasp of certain knowledge needed to learn on the next level. So, a promotional examination is held to insure that you are able to learn on your next level – not to see if you have perfected your previous knowledge.

e. Ranks:

After four to five years of continuous study, the average student will normally earn his Black Belt. This will mean that he is a novice – a beginner. Unknown to many outside of the martial arts, there are ten degrees of black belt. In the Korean martial arts, 1st, 2nd and 3rd degree black belts are advanced students, generally teaching under the guidance of a. 4th, 5th and 6th degree black belt, which are ranks considered to be instructors, or experts. 7th, 8th and 9th degree black belts have earned the title of head / chief instructor, and are considered capable of forming their own martial arts styles (known in Korea as "Kwans", meaning "schools of thought"). Although some may claim the rank, in the Korean martial arts the 10th degree black belt is an honor reserved for exceptional martial artists after their death.

f. Kihap (Yelling):

The yells used in the martial arts serve many important functions. Known in Korean as "*Kihap*", the yells used by martial artists are designed to unite the internal spiritual energy of the martial artists, "*Ki*", with his external physical energy. The word *Kihap* is formed from two Korean words, *Ki*, meaning "energy", and *Hap*, meaning "to combine or coordinate". So, *Kihap* means "to combine or coordinate energy or power". *Kihaps* are used during patterns, sparring, self-defense, breaking and other activities to unite the spiritual and physical energies of the martial artist. *Kihaps* also serve other important functions. During sparring and self-defense, they are used to insure that the abdominal muscles are tensed and able to withstand a blow. They can also be used as self-defense techniques – a sudden loud "*Kihap*" will often cause an attacker to momentarily pause in his attack.

Jeremiah 51:38 They shall roar together like lions: they shall yell as lions' whelps.

1 Samuel 4:5 And when the ark of the covenant of the LORD came into the camp, all Israel shouted with a great shout, so that the earth rang again.

4:6 And when the Philistines heard the noise of the shout, they said, What meaneth the noise of this great shout in the camp of the Hebrews? And they understood that the ark of the LORD was come into the camp.

2 Chronicles 13:15 Then the men of Judah gave a shout: and as the men of Judah shouted, it came to pass, that God smote Jeroboam and all Israel before Abijah and Judah.

Ezra 3:11 And they sang together by course in praising and giving thanks unto the LORD; because he is good, for his mercy endureth for ever toward Israel. And all the people shouted with a great shout, when they praised the LORD, because the foundation of the house of the LORD was laid.

g. Patterns:

Patterns (forms), known in Korea as "*Hyungs*" or "*Poomse*", are prearranged series of movements designed to help students practice their techniques alone and to help standardize techniques among schools. Practicing patterns helps teach the student to focus his attention and to perfect his movements. While practicing patterns, the student should always visualize an opponent. Otherwise, he is just dancing.

Ezra 43:10 Thou son of man, shew the house to the house of Israel, that they may be ashamed of their iniquities: and let them measure the pattern.

1Timothy 1:16 Howbeit for this cause I obtained mercy, that in me first Jesus Christ might shew forth all longsuffering, for a pattern to them which should hereafter believe on him to life everlasting.

Titus 2:7 In all things shewing thyself a pattern of good works: in doctrine shewing uncorruptness, gravity, sincerity,

Hebrews 8:5 Who serve unto the example and shadow of heavenly things, as Moses was admonished of God when he was about to make the tabernacle: for, See, saith he, that thou make all things according to the pattern shewed to thee in the mount.

h. Breaking:

Always a favorite part of any martial arts demonstration, board and brick breaking serves an important purpose. It takes proper mental and physical coordination to be able to break properly. If one succeeds in breaking one inch of wood, then one should train harder and plan to be able to break two inches the next time. Breaking demonstrates an ability to generate and focus adequate physical power as well as proper mental focus.

(If you are doing a breaking demonstration as an evangelistic event, remember that ultimately, it is the Word of God that is the best demonstration. By depending on it, the minister will see the sinner's heart broken).

Jeremiah 23:29 Is not my word like as a fire? Saith the LORD; and like a hammer that breaketh the rock in pieces?

i. Sparring:

There are many types of sparring ranging from pre-arranged "one-steps" to full-contact fighting. In all cases the opponent is the same – your own lack of knowledge. In the martial arts, we do not spar with the intention of trying to win, or "beat" our opponent, we spar to improve our own techniques and to learn of and destroy our own limitations.

1Corinthians 9:24 Know ye not that they which run in a race run all, but one receiveth the prize? So run, that ye may obtain.

9:25 And every man that striveth for the mastery is temperate in all things. Now they do it to obtain a corruptible crown; but we an incorruptible.

9:26 I therefore so run, not as uncertainly; so fight I, not as one that beateth the air:

9:27 But I keep under my body, and bring it into subjection: lest that by any means, when I have preached to others, I myself should be a castaway.

j. Tournaments:

Martial arts tournaments can be great fun but should never become more important than proper traditional martial arts practice. Tournaments show one aspect of the martial arts – sport. Self-improvement and self-defense are more important than winning trophies.

k. Violence?

The martial arts often get a bad rap because of the violence involved. Martial arts techniques can cause horrific damage when misused. For this reason, instructors should be very selective about who they accept as students. The martial arts are intended to teach self-defense, self-control, and self-confidence. It is hoped that as a student learns of his potential for destruction, he will also learn of his need for control and discipline.

2Samuel 22:3The God of my rock; in him will I trust: he is my shield, and the horn of my salvation, my high tower, and my refuge, my saviour; thou savest me from violence.

REMEMBER: THERE IS NO HONOR IN DEFEATING A MUCH WEAKER OPPONENT; YOUR REAL OPPONENT IS YOUR OWN LACK OF SELF-CONTROL.

3. Teach the Basics:
Provides the foundation. Like the cornerstones of a skyscraper.

Luke 6:47 Whosoever cometh to me, and heareth my sayings, and doeth them, I will shew you to whom he is like:

6:48 He is like a man which built an house, and digged deep, and laid the foundation on a rock: and when the flood arose, the stream beat vehemently upon that house, and could not shake it: for it was founded upon a rock.

4. Teach one-step sparring:
For practicing your techniques in a controlled atmosphere with a partner.

Proverbs 27:6 Faithful are the wounds of a friend; but the kisses of an enemy are deceitful.

5. Teach Controlled Alternative Free-Sparring:
To build self-control using techniques of block and attack without contact. Like a live Chess game, it stimulates the mind.

Proverbs 27:17 Iron sharpeneth iron; so a man sharpeneth the countenance of his friend.

6. Teach Free Sparring:
To improve reflexes, apply techniques of attack, blocking and counter-attack.

Psalm 144:1 Blessed be the LORD my strength, which teacheth my hands to war, and my fingers to fight:

7. Teach Three Styles of Techniques:
- Competition style–as a sport to acquire trophies and medals.
- Exhibition style–shows beauty, grace and effectiveness.
- Practical style–application for self-defense.

Colossians 4:6 Let your speech be I with grace, seasoned with salt, that ye may know how ye ought to answer every man.

1Corinthians 9:16 For though I preach the gospel, I have nothing to glory of: for necessity is laid upon me; yea, woe is unto me, if I preach not the gospel!

9:17 For if I do this thing willingly, I have a reward: but if against my will, a dispensation of the gospel is committed unto me.

9:18 What is my reward then? Verily that, when I preach the gospel, I may make the gospel of Christ without charge, that I abuse not my power in the gospel.

9:19 For though I be free from all men, yet have I made myself servant unto all, that I might gain the more.

9:20 And unto the Jews I became as a Jew, that I might gain the Jews; to them that are under the law, as under the law, that I might gain them that are under the law;

9:21 To them that are without law, as without law, (being not without law to God, but under the law to Christ,) that I might gain them that are without law.

9:22 To the weak became I as weak, that I might gain the weak: I am made all things to all men, that I might by all means save some.

9:23 And this I do for the gospel's sake, that I might be partaker thereof with you.

8. Teach Breaking Techniques:

Builds self-confidence, shows effectiveness and practical application without possible injury to partner.

2 Samuel 22:35 He teacheth my hands to war; so that a bow of steel is broken by mine arms.

9. Teach Anyone:

Anyone can learn Martial Arts. Regardless of age or sex, it is never too late to begin practice. Even the physically challenged individual can learn martial arts because it is not just kicking and punching. It is a modern universal art of self-defense and character development.

Job 27:11 I will teach you by the hand of God: that which is with the Almighty will I not conceal.

10. Teach Properly Build Speed, Power, and Accuracy.

When you are instructing, have the student begin practicing techniques, always following these basic steps. Have them perform the technique in (5) steps, slowly, and then cut down to only (4) steps. Have them relax as they repeat the technique several times with good balance, then cut their steps down to (3) then (2), then finally have them perform it all on (1) count, smoothly, quickly, powerfully and accurately. Speed, power, and accuracy originate from and depend on the proper form and precise angling of the joints. For maximum power, follow these practicing guidelines when teaching.

Isaiah 28:10 For precept must be upon precept, precept upon precept; line upon line, line upon line;

11. Teach Through Promotional Testing?
- To measure your progress as an instructor.
- For the student to experience the expression of what he has learned.

- To teach true friendship, cooperation and organization.
- To instill a desire to achieve the highest goal.

1Corinthians 9:24 Know ye not that they which run in a race run all, but one receiveth the prize? So run, that ye may obtain.

12. Teach Discipline and Self-Respect

Sometimes in life it becomes necessary to control your actions, though you may wish to express something that seems valuable to you. You should always be aware of what you do and say and how it will affect others. Discipline yourself. When you can control what you do and say, you will know the satisfaction of having contributed your best, whether it is by outward expression or silence at the right time. Your ability to discipline yourself will have a direct effect on the degree of success you have in attempting to reach your goals. Your self-respect will be something that you deserved and earned.

Job 36:10 He openeth also their ear to discipline, and commandeth that they return from iniquity.

13. Teach Patience

"Everything comes to those who wait". When one begins practicing martial arts, hours are spent performing techniques over and over, sweating as you go. When you leave to go home, you can leave that room behind you, but you must take that patience and persistence with you. Not only during practice but also in everything you do, have patience. Whether driving your car or cooking dinner, give yourself the gift of time. Don't try to beat the red light. Patience can save your life.

Romans 5:3 And not only so, but we glory in tribulations also: knowing that tribulation worketh patience;

Isaiah 40:31 But they that wait upon the LORD shall renew their strength; they shall mount up with wings as eagles; they shall run, and not be weary; and they shall walk, and not faint

14. Teach Goal Setting

Whenever you drive your car you must go a certain direction; otherwise you will make unnecessary turns and waste fuel. The same is true in life. You should have a goal, a direction in which you will go. In certain times of hardship, having, keeping and relying on your goal can help brace you for the continuous road ahead.

> *Philippians 3:14 I press toward the mark for the prize of the high calling of God in Christ Jesus.*

15. Teach Promise Keeping

Everyone makes commitments in their life but few people practice the art of keeping their word on promises. Whenever you make a commitment, stick by it, even if circumstances change and you end up losing somewhere. Your promise is your name. Give it a reason to be depended on.

> *1John 2:25 And this is the promise that he hath promised us, even eternal life.*

16. Teach Respect

The meaning of respect includes several things, and all of which deal with your relationship with others. The degree to which you trust, love attempt to understand others, this is the same degree of respect you have for them. If you ignore someone, obviously, your respect for that person is not great. Attempt to extend yourself, to offer your undivided attention so that not only do you please others but you also gain from the experience. Enrich your life by respecting others.

> *Psalm 138:6 Though the LORD be high, yet hath he respect unto the lowly: but the proud he knoweth afar off.*

17. Teach Martial Arts: A Way of Life

Did you eat breakfast today? Probably so. Just as you need to nourish your body everyday, martial arts is also a daily supplement to good health. Also neither with food nor martial arts should you feast and/or famine. You can buy anything you want with money; a car, clothes or a house, but even a million dollars cannot buy your good health.

Luke 4:4 And Jesus answered him, saying, It is written, That man shall not live by bread alone, but by every word of God.

18. Teach Character

One of the most important distinctions between individuals is their character. As children, we are blind to politics, financial and social status. We act how we feel, spontaneously and without influence. As we reach adulthood, we learn the rules of the world and that in some cases, acquiring what you want means sacrificing a little individuality. If we are fortunate enough to begin martial arts as a child, we can avoid the adolescent conformity. Individuality, pride, self-confidence, optimism; none of these are for sale. This is another part of you that a million dollars cannot buy.

Proverbs 20:7 The just man walketh in his integrity: his children are blessed after him.

19. Teach Leadership

To be a good leader one must have a conscious desire to dedicate himself to others and realize his responsibilities and duties to them. He should speak to anyone and everyone on their own level regardless of their position in society: Poor, famous, sick or powerful. People are equal and personal circumstances do not alter their right to count. Empathize. Know hunger if your fellow man is hungry. Create a bond between you and others. A leader is the king of the mountain, but he wants everyone up there with him.

Isaiah 55:4 Behold, I have given him for a witness to the people, a leader and commander to the people.

CHAPTER 12:

GETTING THE ACTUAL

CLASS STARTED

Ministries are usually under-funded, so we will focus on the top ten free promotional events or items of all time that can get your class up and going, or double your enrollments if you already have a class. Many of these techniques have been tried in rural areas, as well as big cities, and small towns. They work.

1. BUSINESS CARD

Your business card should contain the following 7 essential pieces of information:

> Your school name.
> Your name and title.
> School address.
> What you offer.
> Your phone number.
> Your web address.
> Your e-mail address.

Nothing more, nothing less. They don't need to hear about your world or official certification, it is a business card, not a resume. Give your business card to every student and every parent that comes into your class. Let them know that you want them to have your phone number handy so that if they ever have a question about training, or more importantly, about the Lord. Then give them two extra cards and say, "Here are two extra cards for your friends or someone at work who is interested in training or has a child who may interested in training." I Guarantee that you will receive several referrals in the next few days just because they had your card handy to pass along to a friend.

Be sure to send that student or parent a thank you card when someone they refer comes in to join. Also give your card to everyone that you do business or ministry with. Your building manager, your insurance agent, your printer, the guy from the pool cleaning service, the girl that details your car, your Sunday school teachers, AWANA workers, and anyone else that you do business or ministry with a regular basis. Tell them, "If you ever decide to take martial arts or get lessons for your child, give me a call." Now, they might not join today, but every time they run across your card, they will think about it. If someone they know ever mentions martial arts they will have your number handy to give out. This is what we call passive marketing. You should do this all of the time.

2. FREE LESSON OFFERS

I have taught for free for many years, and charged for lessons as well. What has been learned by trial and error is: If it doesn't cost SOMETHING, it is considered useless. Take a page from experience:

" When charging a minimal amount for lessons, I had more students than I could shake a stick at. If they had no money to pay for lessons, they were accepted anyway. Some of the members of the church provided "scholarships", while others were accepted on "work study". They class barely had room to move.

Then people began saying 'you shouldn't charge'. Being a pastor, I decided I would teach for free. What happened? They class virtually disappeared. If it was "FREE", if they had to invest "Nothing", then they quit coming, plain and simple".

If you don't want to "charge" for lessons, there is a third alternative, which has worked well for me. Once a month, ask students to make a "donation" to the church. Come up with a suggested donation per month and let the students know. The money can then be used for purchasing class equipment, paying estimated utilities the class uses if in a church facility (church folks LOVE THIS, make sure to let the congregation know this money is being GIVEN by the martial arts class), or given to missions. Make sure the class knows the ministry needs the donations.

3. BULLETIN BOARDS

Every supermarket, laundry mat, and church in your town has a bulletin board where you can post your flyers or brochures. Also local colleges and public buildings have bulletin boards that you should post on. Use layering when you put them up. Staple one to the bulletin board and then another one over top of it and so on. That way you have several flyers allowing someone to take one for themselves and still have a few left for others to see. The flyer should be on a bright colored paper. This attracts peoples attention to it.

4. SHOW AND TELL

Yes, I am serious. Go to school for show and tell. Better yet, help your students in the next "talent" show. You'll be amazed at the kids that will want to get involved in your class from this simple event.

5. FAMILY & FRIENDS APPRECIATION NIGHT

Give each child invitations that they sign inviting their parents, grandparents or any friend or relative to the event. The invitation should read as follows:

You Are Cordially Invited To FAMILY & FRIENDS APPRECIATION NIGHT
by:_____"child's
name goes here.
After the class finishes their warm up session we will have a special class. You may video tape or take photographs to remember this special night. There will be a special demonstration staring the members of our class.
We look forward to seeing you at this special event.

Signed, The Staff of Your local martial arts school or Church.

When they get to the school or church, have them sign in for a chance to win the Door Prize that will be given away at the end of the class. Have a table set up with coffee, fruit punch, vegetable tray and cookies for the guests to snack on. Set up an area where the students can stand with their favorite instructor and their friend or family member to get their photo taken. (In front of something with your school / church logo in the background would be best. Have them get in line and make sure that everyone gets a chance. Then repeat this by doing some back and forth poses with the students for video taping. Then let grown ups hold the kicking shield during class for the child to kick or hold the focus pads while the child punches. And remind them to take pictures! They will have a blast. Each time we host this event I normally get three or four parents to enroll after being in this fun class with their child. Remember, remind parents that "unlike little league," they can do martial arts class with their child.

Parents talk to coworkers and friends about this event for days and it always provides me with several new referrals. This event is so much fun for me as well as the students. You will look forward to doing it again and again.

CHAPTER 13:

A KARATE FOR CHRIST

TESTIMONY

By David Dunn

My class has a simple purpose statement: *Ridgecrest Karate for Christ exists to glorify God by leading people to become fully devoted followers of Jesus Christ.* A fully devoted follower of Jesus Christ seeks to become a person who daily worships God, brings others to Christ, learns God's word, loves other believers, and serves in the world. *This is the heart and soul of what we are trying to accomplish. This is Karate for Christ!*

Starting your own Karate for Christ ministry can be very rewarding. But like anything, it has its up and downs. If you are considering starting this type of ministry, I would like to share words of encouragement and some things that have helped me learn and grow.

Fall 2001 I caught the vision for Karate for Christ when I saw the opportunity to reach others for Christ by doing something I enjoy. We launched our classes that summer. I soon discovered that when you reach out to others for Jesus, you come under spiritual attack. Satan will try to discourage you or destroy what you are doing. Just as we teach our students to memorize Scripture, we need to do the same, because God's word is our sword. A master swordsman practices his art daily. Likewise, we should study God's word daily.

1Corinthians 15:58 Therefore, my beloved brethren, be ye stedfast, unmoveable, always abounding in the work of the Lord, forasmuch as ye know that your labour is not in vain in the Lord.

When I started teaching Karate for Christ, I was full of enthusiasm and energy. Later on I began to wonder if it was worth it. Every week I had to move tables and chairs out of our fellowship center. After that I swept the floor and hauled borrowed training mats into class. I was financially struggling and feeling physically exhausted. Also, I was not getting much support from my church. I began to have doubts about what I was doing, and I didn't think I was making a difference for Jesus.

Philippians 4:6 Be careful for nothing; but in every thing by prayer and supplication with thanksgiving let your requests be made known unto God. 7 And the peace of God, which passeth all understanding, shall keep your hearts and minds through Christ Jesus.

It was during one of my low points that God started showing me some of the fruit from our Karate for Christ ministry. A boy from a non-Christian family joined my class. He is a great kid and loves martial arts. But I noticed that during our devotion and prayer time he seemed to be in a different world. I realized this might be his first exposure to Christianity, Bible study and prayer. Then one day after he had attended several weeks, I asked for prayer requests and he raised his hand. He asked me to pray for his grandmother because she was sick. This was a breakthrough that he was actually participating.

A few weeks later I was doing another devotion and prayer time with the 8 to 12-year-old boys. During prayer requests, the same little boy asked me to pray that his dad would quit smoking. Another boy asked the same thing for his dad. Then another boy asked if I would pray for his dad to quit drinking. This touched my heart, and I could sense God saying to me, "Stick with this because the ministry is making a difference." He will show you the same things if you look for them. I kept working with these boys. They were doing a good job on their yellow belt material and approaching a test date. At the end of our class I reminded everyone that they needed to know John 3:16 for their promotion. The next week one of the non-churchgoing mothers came to me with her Bible and asked me where to find the verse. I replied, "In the Gospel of John, John 3:16." Later I realized that she had wanted me to show her exactly where it was in the Bible.

Everything worked out, though. The very next week while I was outside unloading the mats, her boy came to me and said, "Mr. Dunn, Mr. Dunn I want to tell you my verse." I listened as he recited, "John 3:16, For God so loved the world, that he gave his only begotten Son, that whosoever believeth in him should not perish, but have everlasting life, John 3:16." I gave him the high five and praised him for doing a good job. Inside the building the same kid ran up and repeated, "Mr. Dunn, Mr. Dunn I want to tell you my verse." This happened about three times. On my last trip out to the van I stopped on the stairs by myself. I choked up as the thought came to me that now his mom knows the verse and maybe his dad. Thank you Lord.

Isaiah 55:11 So shall my word be that goeth forth out of my mouth: it shall not return unto me void, but it shall accomplish that which I please, and it shall prosper in the thing whereto I sent it.

God used this little boy to show me my toil was not in vain. He allowed me to see through these small things that he was painting a big picture of more exciting things to come. If each one of our clubs can make a small difference, together we can make a big difference.

August 2003, we were privileged to have Dr. Daryl R. Covington as our guest instructor. Dr. Covington is a 7th Degree Black Belt in Shinsei Hapkido, the director of the Shinsei Hapkido Federation and the Vice President of Karate for Christ International. He taught a three-hour seminar at Ridgecrest Karate for Christ. When we originally set up the meeting, I asked him to close with an altar call. We agreed to pray about this two weeks before the visit. I had also shared the John 3:16 story with our activity minister Mr. Randy Akers, who became more interested in Karate for Christ and attended our seminar. During the last thirty minutes of the seminar, Dr. Covington did some preaching and gave an invitation to receive Jesus as Savior. Two young boys raised their hands. Glory to God! Mr. Akers saw that this was more than just a karate class. After that night, my church began to support us as a ministry. We started receiving nice write-ups in the church bulletin and in the activities directory.

Whenever fellow believers inquired about Karate for Christ, I took the opportunity to share the John 3:16 story and our need for mats. God used this to help our class. Just before our seminar, I received a phone call from a brother in my "Faith Family" Sunday School class. He told me that fund-raising isn't something that he would normally do, but God put it on his heart to help raise funds to purchase mats for Ridgecrest Karate for Christ. When I heard those words, I was in the state of unbelief for a minute. Then I realized God was using some of my Christian friends to help us. This impacted my life and increased my faith, and God started becoming more real to me than ever before.

The same weekend as the seminar my friend made his presentation to our class. I received a call later that day and was told that my entire Faith Family had agreed to make Karate for Christ mats a class project. They said they would raise the money needed in a matter of weeks. That call alone was a very special blessing, because it meant that my friends, my Faith Family, and my church were joining as partners in Ridgecrest Karate for Christ. They wanted us to have the tools to reach others for Jesus Christ!

At our next Karate for Christ class, I shared this news with my students. To my surprise, a student approached me and said that he felt led to help buy the mats. As we talked, he handed me a folded up check. I thought it might be twenty-five or fifty dollars, but I decided I'd better look at it before the man left. As I opened the check, I almost fell over. This wonderful Christian had donated $600. I was tearful and had a hard time talking. All I could do was give this Christian brother a hug and a big "thank you." About eight weeks later we had our mats ordered. In the end about $3400 was raised and we were able to buy several high-quality mats to cover a 24 by 30 foot area. God supplied our needs according to his riches in Christ Jesus!

Luke 10:2 Therefore said he unto them, The harvest truly is great, but the laborers are few: pray ye therefore the Lord of the harvest, that he would send forth laborers into his harvest.

This is a great verse to meditate on. You can make a difference in some-one's life too. If you start your own Karate for Christ ministry you will be taking on the responsibility of being a teacher, and you need to do this with a servant's heart. Always try to set a good example in everything you do.

Go to the Karate for Christ website and you will find many ideas for starting a ministry. Also read the "About Us" information. Adapt ideas and suggestions as your guidelines, because the way we teach martial arts will vary from style to style. Our common bond is Jesus Christ, regardless of which martial arts system we teach. Our students need to understand we get our real power and protection from him. Glorify God, share the good news, and prepare our youth to be the Christian leaders of the future. If you're not teaching Karate for Christ, it's just karate.

CHAPTER 14:

TEACHING SPECIAL

NEEDS KIDS

By Charlaine Englehardt

Anyone can learn martial arts. The arts are hidden within the person. Sometimes it just takes a good Sensei to carve away the obstructions to show the person the art that lies within. Daryl Covington made the following statement, "When I was teaching in Kentucky, we had a young student the school system claimed was unteachable. They could do nothing with him. Surprisingly enough, in just a few short weeks of class, this young student began to excel and learn at an amazing rate. What had been the school's problem? Why couldn't they teach him?

Unfortunately, they are not alone in their lack of experience dealing with ADD. Children with Attention Deficit Disorder (ADD) are common to see in martial arts schools. The structure, discipline, broad range of physical movements, and even the built-in consequences have been recommended by doctors, psychiatrists, psychologists, and teachers who work these highly distractable young people.

We are the parents of such a young man. *Tae Kwon Do* was recommended for him by his teacher, who had previously worked with several students with ADD/ADHD. A co-worker of my husband taught in a community program. Our son did a lot of pushups and wall sits. The instructor did not believe in ADD nor in the usage of medication for ADD. But he did know that it was important to get his eye contact when giving verbal instruction. Unfortunately, many instructors are poorly trained to help these students with their unique set of difficulties. Even worse, those in children and youth ministries are not any better trained. Those trusted by parents to aid in the spiritual growth of youth with ADD, who do not know how to work with the special needs, can hurt rather than help their walk with Christ. Worse, youth can be turned off to know Christ altogether because of a harsh or aloof leader.

Children with ADD and ADHD can be a tremendous challenge, but we as Christian martial arts instructors can help these individuals learn how to use a special gift that God has given them. Children with Attention Deficit Disorder (with or without hyperactivity) have a tremendous potential we can bring out in them. Unfortunately, it does not appear this way when we first encounter them. They appear to be whirlwinds bent on destruction and chaos, promising to be a real headache the moment they enter the doors of our ministries. Their parents are frustrated and exhausted, yet very protective. They hope we can instill some discipline into these wiggly, squirmy children. But they also feel sorry for their little ones when they are being corrected for the zillionth time.

Yet inside these little powerhouses is a unique grouping of gifts, talents, and abilities yet to be discovered, harnessed, then used for the glory of God. We have to look for the diamonds in the rough. The rough parts you see are not socially acceptable nor endearing. Other children and many adults are offended by the lack of personal space left when these children approach them at full volume. They also seem to be a year or two behind their peers socially and emotionally.

Our son related best with children two to three years younger than himself. The nervous motor tics tend to drive everyone nuts (you probably know those who have to bounce their legs or drum their fingers). How about the kid who ate paste in school? They usually forget to comb their hair, brush their teeth, get their clothes dirty checking on something outside, and later to put on deodorant.

Sometimes ADD is accompanied by learning disabilities, Tourette's Syndrome (verbal outbursts), functional autism, or epilepsy. These further complicate their situations. Their wonderful, sunny outlook on life changes to that of anger or fear because of the ill treatment they receive from other people. This can also be a result from the treatment their parents give them because of a lack of understanding or unwillingness to have a label put on their child.

Many ADD/ADHD students are not diagnosed formally. Even on medication, these behaviors are still present, but not as drastic as untreated. Many symptoms can become positive assets. One of the first things you will notice when you meet someone with ADD/ADHD is that they are looking around rather than at you when you speak with them. There are so many thoughts running through their minds vying for attention. But one of the most obscure things can draw their attention immediately. If it happens to be of tremendous interest, it is nearly impossible to bring their attention back. They interrupt with subjects that do not pertain to anything going on. They are extra sensitive to minor pain and very easily upset emotionally, letting out a loud howl that would wake the dead.

A blessing from God? Or a major migraine? Before you get out the headache tablets, let's look at some of the symptoms again with the flip side, which God can use:

1. Their distractibility can actually become the ability to multi-task more than the average person. Our son was not paying attention to a thing the *Tae Kwon Do* instructor was teaching when it came to sparring or so we thought. I could not look as Seth approached the instructor to face a boy almost twice his weight. The parents of this large lad encouraged him to beat our son to a pulp, which is what I was afraid would happen. Instead, he used what was taught previously to hold his own against his opponent. He had heard the instructions. People with ADD tend to have several projects going on at once and can tell you in tremendous detail about each one.

2. The distractibility that draws them to dart somewhere else can become an immediate reaction in an emergency situation. Many people are afraid that those with ADD would be the last ones to rely upon with emergency situations. However, there have been several situations reported in newspapers about those who are teens and young adults immediately seeing a dangerous situation and responding before other people nearby even noticed there was a problem. They tend to notice the obscure. Instead of seeing the superficial, they tend to notice aspects of people and situations, which tend to be covered by frills, diversion, and deception. But yet they cannot see the subtleties of sarcasm by their peers who mock them at school because they are different or weird. I would prefer to have someone like this in charge of my class when I have to be out.

3. Their curiosity is a sign of their high intelligence. This intelligence

is usually in the gifted level when tested. Do the ADD children you know break things when they are simply looking at them? It is usually because they are looking at the texture, how something is made, and all the other aspects of the things that end up broken. They are not purposely being destructive! Most 2 year olds with ADD can say words like dinosaur. These children are the engineers, artists, musicians, pastors, and youth leaders who are not willing to accept the status quo or to stay boxed in. They are the ones who find innovative ways to improve things around them or find another way of doing the mundane. Instructors in karate classes with ADD/ADHD come up with some of the best drills and varied ways of teaching the same thing. They also find a variety of self-defense techniques some of us would not think of.

4. Teaching these special children takes a different approach from other students in our ministries. So, how can we help these diamonds in the rough? Find ways to build self-respect, downplay attention to unusual behavior, and break down skills into one or two steps at a time. Here are some things that work well for us:

Work with parents to find universal signals the student will recognize and respond to in order to gain his or her attention. Don't constantly say the child s name. Snapping your fingers just before the signal should help. Make sure the student knows what you will be doing.

Keep instructions short! The Indianapolis 500 of thoughts is going on in that little head. You have to wedge in the information between thoughts. If you must give a list, keep it to one or two items. Otherwise, the last thing you say is all you will get. Walk around and through the students as you help and correct.

When you discover a pattern of difficulties (i.e. directional confusion or coordination problems), keep the verbal instruction directed to the general group, then only give one or two corrections as you physically help the child achieve the task. Catch him or her doing something right. They are constantly being yelled at, corrected, or criticized. Remember that it takes only 1 negative to erase 5 positives for these children. Instead, tell them something positive first, give the correction, then finish when possible with the positive of the correction they make.

Do not expect them to stand perfectly still! This is impossible. However, you can give them limited boundaries of movement. Allow small fidgets, but calm down big ones which can cause a disruption with the flow of the class.

Since ADD children tend to misplace things, have one specific place for them to put their mouth guards, equipment, and Bibles. Encourage them to have a bag to put these things in and one place at home that this bag is stored. This should help the student to be prepared for class 90% of the time. For the other 10%, find a reasonable negative consequence to remind them to bring their things, then remind them how they can accomplish this task. Encourage parents to use Velcro to keep the gi top closed! Tape or double tie the drawstring on the pants! Check their belts at the door and help tie them correctly so that these students do not come unraveled. Enforce the rules immediately. Remind the students how to stay within the rules.

Do not allow other students to pick on this child. Remind them that we are to treat other people the way we want to be treated. Let them know that the ADD child has problems and that patience is essential. Distract bullies in the class early before the ADD student realizes what is happening. Give them a task they can do well to help you. Everyone needs to feel needed and wanted. Have them pass out equipment, read the memory verse, or anything they will only succeed at doing. Have your higher rank ADD students be a buddy to a new student on the first day. Give them tasks as helpers that will help the others students look up to them. Recognize that the aggravation you feel is also what your students feel. They will drain and frustrate you. Wait until they leave to vent frustration.

Talk with your pastor, a trusted adult, or work out your frustration through your own martial arts workout. Do not lash out at the child! Listen to the students and instructors in your classes who are also frustrated. Acknowledge it and give alternatives to help them deal effectively with the ADD/ADHD students. These types of behavior patterns and symptoms in children tend to target them for abuse by those who cannot control their tempers. Remember that these children are specially created by God just they way they are; they are not damaged or mentally handicapped. They simply have a hidden disability (a neurological disorder) and function differently than the average. ADD/ADHD children have a special gift from God that they just do not know how to use yet. It is our job for our Lord to help them learn how to use it.

Build a support network within your classes for these students. Give them buddies, but rotate the buddies, to help them. Have different instructors work with them when possible. This will help alleviate aggravation and burnout. They will also have the opportunity to find those things that work for them to learn what you have to teach them. Since the right and left sides of the brain are not communicating as well as they should, this approach will help both hemispheres process the information more effectively. Different teaching styles aid varied learning styles which may exist in just one ADD student. Their parents are struggling with the disorder, too. The parents already hear so much negativity about the child s behavior. Many feel like they have failed as parents or have done something wrong. Give them the positive first. Only share what is important that was a problem.

Forget the small stuff. Things like chewing on the belt is not newsworthy whereas, punching someone who has pestered him is. Encourage those who have not had their children diagnosed to have a professional help them pinpoint the problem and give them a treatment plan. Put yourself in the parents' shoes, so to speak, this will help keep things in perspective. The confusing bundles of energy who come into your classes are diamonds in the rough. The Lord brings them to us because we are to be used by Him to help them become wonderful, fruitful children of God. You must be the one to do this because the Lord led them to your ministry.

CHAPTER 15:

TEACHING KIDS IN

GENERAL

By Chris Dewey

Why will the martial arts help my child?

On the face of it, this seems like a simple enough question. It is also a question I am asked frequently by parents of prospective students. I have thought long and hard about this question. I can tell you all the rote answers like: helping your child to learn focus, self-control, responsibility, self discipline, a sense of duty, and a sense of caring. I can tell you it will help your child improve his behavior at home and at school; and that grades will often improve. But are these the real answers? I don't think so.

Aristotle gave us the Law of Cause and Effect, and it is to that law we turn to find our real answer. All the benefits I just listed are effects. They are the results of training, just as the kicking and punching skills your child learns are the results of training. So this brings us to a question of what then is the cause of these changes? And how do the martial arts create such effects? The answer lies in the way in which martial arts teaching and learning takes place.

There are two styles of learning: learning is either informational or transformational. Informational learning is typically what goes on in the classroom – a child learns how to spell a word. When it is correct the child gets points on a test, but when it is wrong the child receives no credit. This, in essence, is informational learning.

Transformational learning takes place when a child acquires a piece of information and it has trickle down effects beyond the simple acquisition of the information itself. When we teach a child to kick, the child learns a skill, just as learning to spell correctly is a skill. The difference comes in the arts when we teach a child to kick, we are also giving the child a responsibility: the safety of his training partner.

The kick itself is nothing special, it is just a skill. The requirement to use that skill with the safety of a training partner in mind, is a wholly different matter. The child who does not learn to control his or her kicks quickly discovers that other children will avoid training with him. This is sometimes a tough lesson.

Another lesson which comes fairly quickly is that the child must learn to focus the kick to a specific target and concentrate upon what he is doing in the moment, again because the safety of a training partner is at risk. Children also find out the quality of the practice counts, not only because the child discovers he does not learn as much, but also that sloppy technique prevents a child's partner from learning as well.

So, by teaching something as simple as a kick, we teach something to a child which transforms him. The transformation occurs as the child learns these lessons for himself. Certainly, we discuss these issues in our chat sessions at the end of each class, but the lesson does not sink in until each child makes it personal. In effect, we provide a tool of learning and the child realizes in order to make any serious progress in the martial arts, he must alter how he thinks and how he behaves. The child cannot simply learn a technique and move on to the next one. This is not something we must to do as instructors; it is inherent in the nature of the martial arts themselves.

In summary, training in the martial arts is a transformational process, because each child chooses to change what they are, as they learn. The process is transformational because the changes come as each child makes a commitment to the training and allows the changes to affect other parts of his life. Each child chooses to make the training something special and personal, and therefore reaps huge benefits affecting many other areas of life. Each child makes the training his own special gift.

CHAPTER 16:

MARTIAL ARTS AND

CHRISTIANITY

For most of my life I have been fascinated and involved in the marital arts. When I was first called into the ministry, some people thought I needed to leave behind "the warrior way" as I followed the Lord's will in my life. These people had a false conception of what the "warrior spirit" is all about.

One of the biggest negatives I hear about my involvement and teaching martial arts is that I am merely teaching people how to fight. In reality, I teach students so they do not have to fight. When one is confident in their ability to defend themselves, one does not have to fight to prove this fact. I do not have to fight someone to prove my ability, I have proven my abilities in the Dojang, so those issues are long settled in my heart. The first aspect of self-defense is to learn to avoid confrontation all together. Without that as a foundation, martial arts have lost their art form.

There is a time to stand. A great example of the "warrior spirit" from a Christian perspective can be found in the Bible in II Samuel 23:8-12 in the list of David's mighty men:

23:8 These be the names of the mighty men whom David had: The Tachmonite that sat in the seat, chief among the captains; the same was Adino the Eznite: he lift up his spear against eight hundred, whom he slew at one time.

9 And after him was Eleazar the son of Dodo the Ahohite, one of the three mighty men with David, when they defied the Philistines that were there gathered together to battle, and the men of Israel were gone away:

10 He arose, and smote the Philistines until his hand was weary, and his hand clave unto the sword: and the LORD wrought a great victory that day; and the people returned after him only to spoil.

11 And after him was Shammah the son of Agee the Hararite. And the Philistines were gathered together into a troop, where was a piece of ground full of lentils: and the people fled from the

Philistines.

12 But he stood in the midst of the ground, and defended it, and slew the Philistines: and the LORD wrought a great victory.

The first example of a man with a biblical warrior spirit in this list is Eleazar. He literally stood and fought until his muscles became so contracted that his sword was literally stuck in his hand. I have found individuals that are involved in Christian martial arts develop this spirit of Eleazar; they are willing to stand until the end and work for God with all their might. In this day and age when most people have the remote control frozen to their hand, we need men and women of God to develop this warrior spirit so exemplified in Eleazar so that we may shake the gates of hell for the glory of God.

Let us turn our focus on the "warrior spirit and Christianity" to a man named Shammah, for he exemplifies the Christian martial artist. The Bible says when everyone else had run away, Shammah stood "in the midst". I have found that martial arts instills in individuals the self confidence needed to take a stand "in the midst". In today's world, many Christians try to straddle the fence and keep both sides happy. One that is taught to have confidence in God through Christian martial arts is highly more likely to take a stand in the midst of tragedy, when the non-warriors have long been gone.

Shammah stood "during the crisis". It is easy to stand when all is well. Martial artists are taught to stand when all is not well. The principle of "mind like water" in Hapkido is a fine example of thinking rationally when the circumstances are irrational.

This is a reference to the mentality one experiences when facing an actual opponent. It means to make the mind calm, like that of an undisturbed body of water. Smooth water reflects accurately the image of all objects within its range, and if the mind is kept calm, the comprehension of the opponent's movements, both psychological and physical, will be both immediate and accurate. If this can take place, then one's responses, both defensive and offensive, will be appropriate and adequate. On the other side of "mind like water", if the surface of the water is disturbed, the images it reflects will be distorted. In other words, if the mind is preoccupied with thoughts of attack and defense it will not properly comprehend the opponent's intentions creating an opportunity for the opponent to attack. When something enters our mind that disrupts this peace, it is like throwing a rock in a still lake. In order to use the "mind like water" principle to our benefit, one must allow that lake to be free of ripples. Water also other properties. Water can be quite destructive. In fact, over time, water is one of the most destructive forces on earth. Your mind must be like water. When necessary, be as destructive as you must, be no more than you need to be.

In a more physical sense, the water principle is the essence of the Hapkido art. Water always follows the most efficient path to its end. It cannot do otherwise! As the water runs its course, barriers and obstacles arise, which at first, appear to impede or slow the flow of the water. Understanding this can lead to the better understanding of Hapkido. On the surface water represents a gentle for of energy, always yielding, always conforming and soft, but yet, water is the shaper of nature. It shapes the mountains and canyons. The first level of understanding the water principle in its Hapkido application invokes the concept that even while yielding to our opponent's strength, we embrace him and his directed energy which in the end, dilutes his attack and focus. When an opponent thrusts, we recede, when he retreats, we fill in the space, just as water does. This is the water principle. Though we are separate from our opponent, by applying the water principle, our movement becomes one with his. We, together, are one. Each apart, but each causing the movement of the other. In the end, there is only the flow, the one movement, the principle of water. There is a greater level of understanding of the water principle as well. Water is free to flow in any direction, so the possibilities are limitless, but, in the end, water always chooses the most efficient path, regardless of terrain or obstacles. Water cannot make the wrong choice about its course of flow. To properly apply the water principle in Hapkido, the martial artist must be on an endless journey to flow to the sea. Like flowing water, if the martial artist takes on this journey any choice he makes and any path he undertakes will bring him closer to his goal, if applying the water principle. Success and failure both become obstacles to flow past in the journey. An advanced application of the water principle is when we can become as water, totally fluid and integrated will all our surroundings. The martial artist does not learn the water principle, he experiences it, becomes it, and expresses it, thus entering the flow.

There is a crisis in our country in a spiritual manner. 3 of 4 Americans do not believe in absolute truth. We teach evolution and wonder why kids act like wild animals. The crisis is deeper than these examples, for it runs deep into the heart of American Christianity.

Within the Southern Baptist Convention alone, 70 % of the Churches are plateaued or declining. Only 4% of all Baptists have ever shared faith. Last year, in the Southern Baptist Convention, 10,000 churches saw no baptisms. That is 1,040,000 sermons, 520,000 prayer meetings, 4,000,000 hymns, and well over 200 million in offerings, and not one soul was reached. These statistics exist in a nation where we have 45 Million teens, of which 44 ½ million do not attend church.

Yes, there is a crisis in Christianity in the God Blessed USA. Passive Christianity is the cause. The great need in this country is to instill a little "warrior spirit" in the youth of our community so they will not bend, bow, or budge to the system of this world and can stand firm on the principles of God's Word. This is what Christian martial arts can be used to do, build the X generation to be warriors for Christ.

The interesting thing about Shammah was "why he stood". He was not defending all of Israel, the Holy City, the Ark of the Covenant, or the King. He was fighting to defend a "field full of lentils"; a pea patch! Fighting by himself, when the whole army fled, Shammah defeated the whole Philistine army, over a pea patch! Why? Because they were God's peas. We learn from Shammah the biblical concept of the warrior spirit, "If it is God's, It is worth fighting for".

In today's society, many companies spend as much as 75% of their advertising budgets to sell their goods to the youth of our country. The average church spends less than 1% of its total budget trying to reach the nation's youth for the sake of Christ. I believe our youth are worth fighting for. In my years of ministry, I have been able to reach more kids with the gospel through marital arts ministry than I have through Sunday School. Without exception, the kids that have been reached through the martial arts ministry, and adults, have become radical Christians that turned the community upside down for Jesus. Why? The warrior spirit. Let's suit up for battle and shake the gates of hell.

CHAPTER 17:

MARTIAL ARTS AND

MEDITATION

Meditation is a biblical concept. Psalm 119:15-16 says, ***"I will meditate in thy precepts, and have respect unto thy ways. I will delight myself in thy statutes: I will not forget thy word."*** The question we must ask is, "What is acceptable meditation?" Much of what goes on in training halls, dojos, dojangs, and schools in the name of "Martial Arts Meditation" is unbiblical. Most of the Eastern forms of meditation, whether up front or behind the scenes, have a common denominator in that they teach we are all part of an impersonal universe. They teach to get rid of the personal things in order to get to be one with the impersonal universe. This is the "empty yourself" or "empty your mind" concept that many martial arts instructors have their students participate in.

Yoga meditation teaches the student to become "one with the impersonal universe". Yoga is a Sanskirt word that literally means to become "One with God". Through yoga and Zen meditation, the concept is to be absorbed into the universe. This in not the road to peace! We cannot find inner peace without first knowing the peace that can only come from the Prince of Peace, Jesus Christ.

What is true meditation? In a biblical perspective, it is a conscious, intelligent use of the mind to learn or study something. True meditation is founded upon the nature and character of God. God loved us enough to send Jesus to cover our sins. We do not need to empty our minds, we need to fill our minds with and meditate on the fact that God loved us enough to sacrifice His son for our sins so that we could have fellowship with Him. God considers us more valuable than anything in this creation. We must meditate on the great love of God.

Secondly, we discover that true meditation is grounded in God's Word. Psalm 1:2 says, ***"But his delight is in the law of the LORD; and in his law doth he meditate day and night"***. Ps 119:97 says, ***"O how love I thy law! It is my meditation all the day"***. ***True meditation is to study God's Word, and then apply it to ones life"***.

Thirdly, true meditation is centered in Jesus Christ. Colossians 2:2-3 says, ***"That their hearts might be comforted, being knit together in*** *love, and unto all riches of the full assurance of understanding, to the acknowledgment of the mystery of God, and of the Father, and of Christ; In whom are hid all the treasures of wisdom and knowledge."* This is the key understanding. We don't empty ourselves to find peace. Peace comes from God. Colossians 3:15-16a says, *"And let the peace of God rule in your hearts, to the which also ye are called in one body; and be ye thankful. Let the word of Christ dwell in you richly in all wisdom".* Peace is only through the shed blood of Jesus Christ. We don't descend into the universe for peace, we look to heaven for our peace. We must fix our minds on Christ (as Isaiah reminds us), not on "nothingness".

There is a great difference between Eastern meditation and Christian meditation. Christian meditation is not a technique, it is a continual lifestyle of Godliness. Psalm 46:10 says, *"Be still, and know that I am God".* We must realize this: We must learn to meditate on God at all times, and even in the midst of adversity, we must be still and look for God in the situation. This is the ultimate result of our biblical meditation.

CHAPTER 18:

DISCIPLESHIP IN

MARTIAL ARTS

We must then, as Christian martial artists, use our art to help disciple the students. Students must learn this lifestyle meditation as a way to deal with life, others, and all circumstances. Each class I teach, I began with prayer and a Bible study. Instead of giving the students the command "mook yum" (meditate), we simply sit down and have a devotional time together, thus spiritually equipping the "warriors" before the "physical" equipping begins. Have Students keep a journal of notes from the devotions and require them to turn it in prior to their belt test. Students that do not keep an updated journal do not belt test. Our classes should be un-apologetically Christian.

There are many great resources for developing a biblical meditation / discipleship program in your school. Feel free to contact me for any recommendations, at <u>drdarylrcovington@yahoo.com</u>, or <u>karateforchristinternational@yahoo</u>.com

CHAPTER 19:

CHRISTIAN SELF

DEFENSE?

A martial arts ministry may require more discipline than other ministries, but this discipline will reflect throughout other church programs as well. I have seen discipline become less and less of a problem in the children's ministries of a local church as more and more children get involved in the martial arts ministry.

A great misconception many get is the idea that Christians are not supposed to defend themselves. This is biblically incorrect. I realize the Bible teaches to turn the other cheek in Matthew 5:38-39, but we must interpret Scripture with Scripture. God warns us not to be vigilantes, and take the law into our own hands, but never does he say "not to defend ourselves". That is a gross misinterpretation of the Word. Donald Englehart says:

Jesus warns us not to continue in anger and the motive for insulting a brother as being subject to judgment similar to the judgment for murder. As for the lesson on wanting revenge, Jesus taught that we should not desire to trade injury for injury, or to take up challenges, but to resolve the conflict. Jesus then continues with not being like the world, but to be more forgiving and caring for the poor. Then His teaching on prayer, fasting, allegiance, worry, etc. In this rather lengthy passage the idea of being a victim was not presented. We are to rejoice at persecution, but persecution has to do with our relationship with Jesus, not our wallet, car, skin color, being in the wrong place at the wrong time, or the clothes we wear; being mugged is not persecution. We see in Scripture that Jesus, who is our example, he did not allow himself to be a victim. Jesus was pursued by a crowd who desired to throw him from a cliff (Luke 4:28-30), but He passed through them and went on His way. This showed us that Jesus did defend Himself until the time had come to complete the task on the cross...The meaning of meek from the Greek text is gentle or humble, not weak or passive, but unfortunately our modern dictionaries have it as being weak spirited and yielding easily. Do you see Jesus encouraging weakness of spirit? Of course not. The humble do not boast and the gentle are not forceful. Jesus is the primary example of meekness and could not be mistaken as weak. Jesus was a carpenter, and would have had the physical stature of one in that trade. Jesus demonstrated His physical strength when he drove the money changers and merchants from the Temple (John 2:14-16). The passage that exalts the meek also exalts the peacemakers, who will be called the sons of God (Matthew 5:9). Allowing ourselves to be victims does not assist in creating peace, but permits the violence to continue. We will be at peace with our fellow man as far as it depends on us (Romans 12:18), but we also realize that sometimes it is not our decision.

To this statement I say, "Amen", and "I agree". Many say Christians cannot serve in the military, for the Ten Commandments say "Thou shalt not kill", but dear friend, God himself sent people to war. We must realize the context of biblical statements before we form unbiblical opinions.

There is no conflict in existence between martial arts and ministry, as long as the martial arts are taught in a Christian environment, free from Eastern mysticism. May we all become "warriors for Christ" and honor the Master in all we do. This is what the Shinse system is all about.

CHAPTER 20:

FALSE TEACHERS

(Contributed)

It seems the Martial arts community is filled with folks just like the churches were in the time of the apostle Paul. Consider the teachings of II Corinthians. False teachers have come into the city of Corinth and they've torn up the church and created all kinds of problems. The people have bought into their deception and their lies, which, of course, has brought great grief upon the heart of Paul. So, what you have in the backdrop of this whole epistle is these false teachers against which Paul is comparing his own right view of ministry because they obviously represent completely the wrong view.

When I sat down and just started writing out characteristics of false teachers, these are the things that showed up on my list: pride, selfishness, deception, irreverence, and destruction. Those would be probably the first five features of false teachers that would be on my list of the, say, a dozen or so, characteristics: pride, selfishness, deception, irreverence, and destructiveness or destruction.

1. False teachers are proud. They are concerned for their own popularity. They are concerned for their own fame. They are concerned for their own notoriety. They are concerned for their own prestige. They're concerned to see themselves and hear themselves in the public eye. They want large crowds, as it were, to bow down in great homage to them. They're characterized by pride and they will do anything to gain the ground they need to gain for the welfare of their own personal ego, including any amount of compromise necessary.

2. Secondly, false teachers are characterized by selfishness. They tend to be self-centered. They are concerned for their own comfort. They are concerned for their own popularity. They are concerned for their own prosperity. In the end, it's all about money, fame, rank papers, and prestige and notoriety equals an increased bank account or an increased self view. They are in it for the money, the fame, or just to show off; its about self to them, trying to be "bigger than life", and the personal material benefits that they can gain as they endeavor to

feed their selfish desires.

3. Thirdly, They are characterized by deception. They usually can weave a very sophisticated web of deception in their teaching because they tend to be articulate, if they're going to be successful, and they endeavor to engage other people to aid them in their deceitful enterprise which gives it the, sort of, I of credibility. In other words, lots of paper, little technique.

4. They're not only proud and selfish and deceptive, but fourthly, they're irreverent. If there's anything that sort of dominates in my thinking about false teachers, it is their irreverence. They have absolutely no regard for the arts. The fact that they would go against the integrity of the arts, that they would elevate themselves the way they do, that they would pervert the truth indicates their utter irreverence. They have little, if any, regard for honor, integrity, respect, discipline, or truth.

5. Finally, they are spiritually destructive. They seek to use people; they seek to abuse people. They seek to lead people into error, which destroys them, brings then into sin, which pollutes them. As you look at false teachers with regard to the world, they are proud and they seek fame and popularity. With regard to themselves, they are self-centered, selfish, self-aggrandizing, self-gratifying. With regard to the nature of their ministry, they are dishonest and deceptive and lack integrity. With regard to the Martial Arts, they are utterly irreverent; in fact, they are not artists, they are counterfeiters, selling paintings for their own that others should get credit for. And, with regard to the people that they influence, they are spiritually destructive. Their relationship to the world, their relationship to the ministry, their relationship to themselves, their relationship to the arts, their relationship to their people all reflects the deviation of their hearts. On the other hand, if you were to write a list of characteristics of the true minister, a true *sensei*, a true shepherd, a true *Kwan Jang Nim, Sa Bu Nim*, or teacher, you would start by saying he is humble and then you probably would say he is lovingly sacrificial, instead of selfish. He is honest and has integrity, rather than deceptive. And, he is reverent

and honors his teachers an the arts, rather than being irreverent. And, he is spiritually strengthening and edifying. You would be right. Remember in II Corinthians, Paul is writing and defining his own attitudes here, against the background of these false teachers whose attitudes should have become obvious to the people in Corinth. A faithful martial artist is humble, unselfish, honest, reverent, and spiritually edifying, just the opposite of false teachers.

What is inside your heart will come out in your art. No one would argue that we live in a world of compromise. In fact, compromise is often touted as a virtue; it's diplomatic and reasonable. On the other hand, those who hold fast their integrity are viewed as difficult, hard-nosed, and unconcerned about the common good. You can understand how the world thinks that way, but shouldn't Christians be different?

Unfortunately, too many believers worry about what people will think, say, or do if they take a stand on godly principles. So instead, they compromise their convictions or maintain them under the cover of darkness. If you're one of those faint-hearted Christians, or if you know people who are, I'd like to encourage you to take a lesson from the life of one man, a man with a backbone.

CHAPTER 20:

SENSEI OR POTENTATE?

Some lawyers and martial arts teachers fancy themselves businessmen, psychologists, philosophers, and rulers. Those notions contrast sharply with what the Bible says about a leader or teacher.

In 2 Timothy 2, for example, Paul uses seven different metaphors to describe the rigors of leadership. He pictures the minister as a teacher (v. 2), a soldier (v. 3), an athlete (v. 5), a farmer (v. 6), a workman (v. 15), a vessel (vv. 20-21), and a slave (v. 24). All those images evoke ideas of sacrifice, labor, service, and hardship. Not one of them makes leadership out to be glamorous, or in the case of the "sensei", a dictatorship. That's because it is not supposed to be glamorous. Leadership in a martial arts setting is not a mantle of status to be conferred, it isn't earned by seniority, purchased with money, or inherited through a system. It doesn't necessarily fall to those who are successful, nor is it doled out on the basis of intelligence or talent. Its requirements are faultless character, spiritual maturity, and above all a willingness to serve humbly.

Our Lord's favorite metaphor for spiritual leadership, a figure He often used to describe Himself, was that of a shepherd–one who tends God's flock. Every martial arts teacher is a shepherd. It is appropriate imagery. A shepherd leads, feeds, nurtures, comforts, corrects, and protects. Those are responsibilities of every teacher in Karate for Christ International.

Shepherds are without status. In most cultures, shepherds occupy the lower rungs of society's ladder. That is fitting. Look at the words of Jesus Christ:

Luke 22:26 But ye shall not be so: but he that is greatest among you, let him be as the younger; and he that is chief, as he that doth serve.

Under the plan God, leadership is a position of humble, loving service. Leadership is *ministry*, not *management*. Those whom God designates leaders are called not to be governing monarchs, but humble slaves; not slick celebrities, but laboring servants. Those who would lead a Karate for Christ class must above all exemplify sacrifice, devotion, submission, and lowliness.

Jesus Himself gave us the pattern when he stooped to wash His disciples' feet, a task that was customarily done only by the lowest of slaves (John 13). If the Lord of the universe would do that, no sensei has a right to think of himself as a bigwig.

Shepherding animals is semi-skilled labor. There are no colleges that offer graduate degrees in shepherding. It isn't that difficult a job. Even a dog can be trained to guard a flock of sheep. In biblical times, young boys–David, for example–herded sheep while the older men did tasks that required more skill and maturity.

Shepherding is not so simple. It takes more than a wandering bumpkin to be a spiritual shepherd. The standards are high, the requirements hard to satisfy. Not everyone can meet the qualifications, and of those who do, few seem to excel at the task. Being a true sensei demands a godly, gifted, multi-skilled man of integrity. Yet he must maintain the perspective and demeanor of a boy shepherd.

With the tremendous responsibility of leading comes potential for either great blessing or great judgment. Good leaders are doubly blessed (1 Tim. 5:17), and poor leaders are doubly chastened (v. 20), James 3:1 says, *"My brethren, be not many masters, knowing that we shall receive the greater condemnation."*

People often ask the secret to Karate for Christ International's success, and how it has grown from a few local students, to over 20,000 worldwide. I'm convinced God's blessing has been on us primarily because our people have shown a strong commitment to biblical leadership. The leaders have endeavored to withstand the preoccupation some martial arts organizations seem to have with self-esteem and the selfishness of our contemporary society.

How are we to minister as teachers? Seek to honor other people and meet their needs. If the people of an organization are fighting for positions of authority, there will be the same kind of chaos as among the disciples when they were arguing over who would be the greatest (Matt. 20:20-21; Mark 9:33-35; Luke 22:24).

We must lead our people humbly. The shepherd determines the direction of the flock. No organization, secular or Christian can be successful if its leaders fail in their task. And no flock can survive and prosper if it shepherds try to trade their staffs for thrones. Put aside your titles, your stripes, your awards, and your ego, and get in there with the sheep Sensei. If you make your students call you Master – STOP.

Also, make sure you realize the Pastor is the spiritual leader of the church's flock. Keep these things in Mind:

1. The church is the only institution Christ promised to build and bless.

2. The corporate functions of the Body all take place in the local church.

3. Preaching is the chief human means God uses to tell of His grace.

4. Your ministry should be accountable to a local church, or don't call it a ministry.

5. Everyone needs a pastor.

CHAPTER 21:

A MAJOR RULE FOR ALL

KFCI MEMBERS

Karate For Christ is a Christian ministries first and foremost, and as such we expect the integrity of our teachers to be of a level that is higher than that of the "world" in general. It is for this reason I wish to remind you and set as policy the following:

No member should list rank they have not worked for. This means no cross ranking, rank trading, free rank, bought rank, rank from an illegitimate organization, style, or person should ever be listed on your site or in your biography.

If you are training with a group that has no established roots or with a friend who has made up a style, it is best not to list any rank. A style is considered to be established if and only if it has a curriculum, a proven track record, and a history that can show it has produced a number of black belts that have gone through the curriculum, and is taught in multiple locations. A "style" being taught at "ONE" school, is NOT a style that is recognized.

If you have a 5th in a style and cross rank in another style which you have not trained in, it is not proper to list the cross ranking. You did not earn it.

If you trade a 4th in one style for a 5th in another similar style, you do not have a 4th and a 5th. That is a promotion, not 15 years spent in 2 separate styles.

Do not trade promotions or rank. That is deceptive.

If your training is eclectic and contains parts of other styles and you wish to pursue or test in those styles, feel free, but test and earn the rank.

Use discretion and honor when listing your ranks and titles.

It is far better to have a rank as a 1st dan and perform as a 4th than the other way around.

Bogus and inferior groups are plentiful. If you do not wish to raise the banner high and proudly, you belong with another group. We do not care if you train or promote in other established styles. We encourage you to gather knowledge and better yourself. All we ask is for you to apply your knowledge and wisdom to your primary style and for its primary purpose.

CHAPTER 22:

KARATE FOR CHRIST

INTERNATIONAL BLACK

BELT PRINCIPLES

1. A black belt must exhibit high personal moral standards.

2. Black belts must be able to concentrate, even in the midst of adversity.

3. Black belts must have control over anger and negative emotions. They develop intense levels of self-control and discipline in all areas of life.

4. Black belts must be respectful and courteous.

5. Black belts do what they are supposed to do on time. Anyone can start a project. Black belts finish the task.

6. Black belts show strong leadership qualities. Leadership training is extremely important in the martial arts. The Christian black belt must show the qualities of a biblical leader.

7. Black belts give back to the martial arts, their church, and their community through service.

8. Students should realize they are working toward the "black belt" the moment they enroll in class. Class requires complete focus and undivided attention. The instructor is not there to make sure you earn your Black Belt, that commitment must come from within.

9. Black Belts enjoy practice and make it a priority. They faithfully attend all classes and compete in all events they are asked to compete in.

10. Black Belts are faithful to writing and keeping a journal of experiences.

11.There is a difference in earning a black belt and achieving the goal of becoming a black belt. To earn a belt, a student simply completes the minimum requirements for the belt rank. After this, he has a belt to wear. To achieve the goal of becoming a Black Belt, the student must train with full intensity and commit his / herself to achieving the excellence necessary to "be" a Black Belt, not just "get" a black belt.

12. Black Belts work as hard on their own than they do in class.

13.The Black Belt exam is a mirror of all your training.

14.Black belts must realize "If every man would help his neighbor, then no man would be without help" –Bruce Lee.

15.Black belts realize where "the Way" leads them: In the maze of pathways In the labyrinth of life We must find the straight and narrow The way that leads to Christ. All other roads are useless The beginning of God's highway Is the cross. – by B. Eisenberg

CHAPTER 23:

QUOTES

This chapter is simply a list of quotes that may serve to motivate you, or be used in your class.

If you follow the present-day world, you will turn your back on the WAY, if you would not turn your back on the WAY, do not follow the world. – Takaun

The only way to judge a Karate Instructor is by his own talent and his ability to teach others to attain a high level of performance – Ken Knudson

You men maybe the greatest martial artists in the world, but can you fight? – Bob Lindsay

Knowing is not enough; we must apply. Willing is not enough; we must do. – Bruce Lee

Pessimism blunts the tools you need to succeed. – Bruce Lee

I count him braver who overcomes his desires than him who conquers his enemies: for the hardest victory is the victory over self. – Aristotle

You must work harder. – Kang Rhee

Anger is a waste of energy. – Jigoro Kano

All work that has eternal reward has to do with people. – Yung Vu

Physical boards are easy to break, it's the mental and physical ones we struggle with. – Daryl Covington

Those who sweat the most during peacetime are those that will bleed the least in war. - Steven R. Barth, IT Assistant

He who chases around after many rabbits ends hungry. – Korean Proverb

The true measure of a man is how he treats someone who can do him absolutely no good. - Samuel Johnson

Do, or do not. There is no 'try'. - Yoda

It okay lose to an opponent, but one must not lose to fear. – Yung Vu

Don't hit at all if it honorably possible to avoid hitting; but never hit soft. - Theodore Roosevelt

The ultimate aim of Karate lies not in victory or defeat, but in the perfection of the character of its participants.
- Master Gichin Funakoshi

To win one hundred victories in one hundred battles is not the highest skill. To subdue the enemy without fighting is the highest skill. – Sun Tzu, the Art of War.

You aren't rich until you have something money can't buy. – Yung Vu

Pain is the best instructor, but no one wants to go to his class.- Choi, Hong Hi, Founder of Taekwon-Do

He who hesitates, meditates in a horizontal position. - Ed Parker

Traditionalists often study what is taught, not what there is to create. - Ed Parker, Grandmaster, American Kenpo.

The first five dan ranks come for what you've gotten out of the system, the next ranks come for what you've given back. – Master Knight.

An unwillingness to deal forcibly with violence does not equate to moral right, nor does passivism bring peace. – Daryl Covington

Staunch traditionalists in the Martial Arts believe that appearance and tradition is everything. To them, technique is nowhere near as important as having the pleats in their hakama straight they die. – D. Covington

It's not just self defense, it's about...self control, body discipline, and mind discipline...It's an art, not a sport. - Elvis Presley.

To become great, you must first sacrifice who you are. – Master Knight.

Hey Sensei. Yes, you with this book in your hand. Think you are a great leader? Turn around and see if anyone is following you. Here are a few thoughts to keep the ego in check:

It is only as we develop others that we permanently succeed. – Harvey S. Firestone

Being in power is like being a lady. If you have to tell people you are, you aren't. – Margaret Thatcher

It's what you learn after you know it all that counts. – John Wooden

Life is not measured by the number of breaths we take, but by the moments that take our breath away. – Joseph Lumpkin

APPENDIX A

BIBLE STUDY STARTERS

FOR CLASS DEVOTIONS

Included here are some basic outlines to help you develop devotional / Bible study curriculum for your martial arts ministry. The first one is purposefully funny.

DEVOTION #1:

HOW TO STAY SAFE IN THE WORLD TODAY

Hebrews 10:24 And let us consider one another to provoke unto love and to good works:

10:25 Not forsaking the assembling of ourselves together, as the manner of some is; but exhorting one another: and so much the more, as ye see the day approaching.

Avoid riding in automobiles because they are responsible for 20% of all fatal accidents.

Do not stay home because 17% of all accidents occur in the home.
Avoid walking on streets or sidewalks because 14% of all accidents occur to pedestrians.

Avoid traveling by air, rail, or water because 16% of all accidents involve these forms of transportation.

Of the remaining 33%, 32% of all deaths occur in Hospitals. Above all else, avoid hospitals.

You will be pleased to learn that only .001% of all deaths occur in worship services in church, and these are usually related to previous physical disorders. Therefore, logic tells us that the safest place for you to be at any given point in time is at church!

Bible study is safe too. The percentage of deaths during Bible study is even less.

FOR SAFETY'S SAKE – Attend church and read your Bible ... IT COULD SAVE YOUR LIFE

From this point on, if time does not allow for the full devotion to be taught, the instructor can teach one point of each of these devotions each week.

DEVOTION # 2:

AP JA SAE (Take a Front Stance) AS GREAT WARRIOR

EPHESIANS 6:10-19

As a Test of Our Character – 1 Samuel 12:24

As a Test of Our Strength – Proverbs 24:10

As a Test of Our Courage – Joshua 1:8-9

As a Test of Our Love – John 14:15

As a Test of Our Faith – Hebrews. 11:1,6

DEVOTION # 3:

HOW SATAN WILL ENTER YOUR DEFENSIVE SPHERE

He Attacks by Mockery – Nehemiah 4:1-6

He Attacks by Conspiracy – Nehemiah 4:7-9

He Attacks by Greed – Nehemiah 5:1-9

He Attacks by Compromise – Nehemiah 6:1-4

He Attacks by Slander – Nehemiah 6:5-9

He Attacks by Treachery – Nehemiah 6:10-14

DEVOTION # 4

TEACHING THE TRADITIONAL KATA OR HYUNG (PATTERNS)

Jeremiah 6:16, Isaiah 58:12

The Pattern of Morality and Virture – Tit. 2:1-8

The Pattern Way of Plain Bible Preaching – Neh. 8:8

The Pattern of Toughness and Contentment – 2 Tim 2:4, Philip. 4:11

The Pattern of Courtesy – Tit. 3:1-4

The Pattern of Hard Work and Dedication – 2 Thess. 3:10

DEVOTION # 5

SOME THINGS WORTH A GOOD FIGHT

2 TIMOTHY 2:1-7

Your Family – Gen. 18:17-19

Freedom – Pro. 29:2

Righteousness – Pro. 14:34

God's Word – Job 23:11-12

Jesus Christ – Acts 1:8

DEVOTION # 6

WHITE BELT SIMPLICITY: SALVATION IS AS EASY AS:

Taking a Bath – Rev. 1:5

Drinking a Glass of Water – John 4:14

Taking a Vacation – Mat. 11:28-30

DEVOTION #7

SENSEI'S WHO ABUSE THEIR POWER

1 Chron. 29:11-12, Psa. 62:11, Rom. 13:1

Sensei is a "karate" word for teacher, for one in charge. Those in "Charge" are often tempted to abuse their power, much like the new black belt. Here are some Bible lessons about "Sensei's" who abused their power.

Preachers sometimes abuse power – 1 Peter 5:1-4

Pretty Women abuse power – Prov. 7:21-27

Parents abuse power – Eph. 6:1-3

Professing Christians abuse power – Acts 1:8-9

DEVOTION #8

WORKING HARD FOR THE BLACK BELT, THE BIBLE WAY

Matthew 21:28, John 9:4, 1 Cor. 3:13-15

If you want to work hard towards the goal of black belt the Bible way, you should:

Stay True to Your Style and Instructor
Always be Willing to Learn
Work Well with Others
Specialize in Your Style
Stay Focused
Remain A Dedicated Student, Even When You Aren't Promoted
Keep Sensei Informed
Always be Available to Help
You Will Be Rewarded for Your Service

DEVOTION # 9

DON'T BRAG ABOUT YOUR RANK

Proverbs 16:19

Actions speak louder than words

If you have to tell others how good you are, you aren't.

Get out of the American Philosophy of life. America is a place where people spend money they don't have, to buy things they don't need, to impress people they don't like

Train hard and let that be enough

Matthew 5:16

DEVOTION #10

WEAPON'S TRAINING: GOD'S TOOLS OF WARFARE

Eccl. 9:18

Tear Down Strongholds – 2 Cor. 10:4

God is our Battle Axe – Jer. 51:20

His Word is Our Sword – Heb. 4:12

DEVOTION #11

GET YOUR SPARRING GEAR ON

(ANALOGY IS MADE USING OLYMPIC TKD SPARRING GEAR)

Chul Sa (Line Up) – Ephesians 6:10 Finally, my brethren, be strong in the Lord, and in the power of his might.

June Be (Ready Stance) – Eph 6:11 Put on the whole armour of God, that ye may be able to stand against the wiles of the devil.

Kung Yea (Address Your Opponent) – Eph 6:12 For we wrestle not against flesh and blood, but against principalities, against powers, against the rulers of the darkness of this world, against spiritual wickedness in high places.

Judge Check All Sparring Gear – Eph 6:13 Wherefore take unto you the whole armour of God, that ye may be able to withstand in the evil day, and having done all, to stand.

Dhe (Belt) – Eph 6:14 Stand therefore, having your loins girt about with truth,

Ho Gu (Chest Protector) – and having on the breastplate of righteousness;

Shin and Instep Pads – Eph 6:15 And your feet shod with the preparation of the gospel of peace;

Forearm Pads for Blocks – Eph 6:16 Above all, taking the shield of faith, wherewith ye shall be able to quench all the fiery darts of the wicked.

Sparring Helmet –Eph 6:17 And take the helmet of salvation, The advantage in a sparring match, use a weapon! – and the sword of the Spirit, which is the word of God:

Be Prepared – Eph 6:18 Praying always with all prayer and supplication in the Spirit, and watching thereunto with all perseverance and supplication for all saints;

DEVOTION #12

KUMDO – SWORD TECHNIQUES

Ephesians 6:17

Using God's Sword, the Bible:

Helps You Get to Know God – Isa. 55:8

Helps You Make Less Errors in Life – Mat. 22:29

Shows God You Care – Psa. 14:2-3

Makes You More Spiritual – John 6:63

Helps Your Fellowship with Believers – James 4:4, Amos 3:3

Makes You Useful – James 1:22

Will Help Establish You to A Strong Christian Testimony – Heb 4:12

Will Make You a Better Witness – Prov. 28:1

Gives Purpose and Direction in Life – Psa 1:1-3

APPENDIX B

THE MARTIAL ARTS

LIBRARY

The following is a non-exhaustive list of Martial Arts books that are a "must" for every serious student of the arts library:

The Book of Five Rings
By Miyamoto Musashi.
I suggest a new translation by Thomas Cleary, which includes *The Book of Family Traditions on the Art of War* by Yagyu Munenori. Written over 350 years ago, this classic is a must. Thomas Cleary's translation makes this classic work easy to understand. The work on the second book included here takes the reader deeper into the warrior tradition.
ISBN 0-7607-0444-9

Living the Martial Way
By Forrest Morgan.
This is a manual for training in warriorship as a life style. It is a great glimpse into the physical discipline and relentless way of the modern warrior. From a Christian perspective, the book seems to be negative against Christianity, but is a good martial arts book. Take it with a grain of salt.
ISBN 0-942637-76-3

Human Anatomy and Physiology
By John W. Hole, Jr.
The choice textbook for many college Anatomy and Physiology courses. Any serious student of the martial arts should own a copy of this work. It amazes me how many so-called "martial artists" have very little knowledge of the human body, and how it works.
ISBN 0-697-05779-8

Weight Training for Martial Artists
By Jennifer Lawler, Ph. D.
This is a complete reference for the martial artist who wants to build strength, power, and speed without sacrificing flexibility. Author Jennifer Lawler has selected only the exercise that will bring maximum results to your martial arts training and organized them into training plans that you can easily customize according to the martial art you practice. Want to improve your speed, strength, flexibility, endurance, upper body power? It is all here, plus tips on selecting the right equipment, lifting correctly, avoiding injuries, and getting the most out of every workout.
ISBN 1-880336-23-5

The Warrior's Heart Revealed
By Joseph Lumpkin and Daryl R. Covington.
This is the defining work on the Philosophy and Methods of Shinse

Hapkido. The book includes Scripture memory plans for your class, kids programs, jr. programs, and essay by some of the greatest martial artist alive, including Erle Montaigue, Richard Hackworth, and others. It has work out programs, drills, and techniques. It is the total package. Erle Montaigue writes: Far too many books written about karate and the martial arts place emphasis only upon the killing aspects and, worse still, upon the 'seeing who is better' aspects of the art. This book does not. In fact, it reflects upon the martial arts from a different time and place, as it was hundreds of years ago, before they became popular in the West and people were awarded ranks in astonishingly short periods of time. This book speaks of the true spirit of the martial arts... when it should be used and when it shouldn't, and recounts the history of a number of mainstream martial arts, and then goes on to put forth the philosophy of 'Christians In the Martial Arts'.

Kodokan Judo
By Jigoro Kano.
Covering everything from the fundamental techniques to prearranged formal exercises for men and women, this book offered detailed explanations of how techniques are combined. The is the comprehensive and most authoritative guide to the martial art of JUDO. Fully illustrated throughout, it will help the student and instructor to discover the principles, techniques, and spirit of this popular art. This is a must have for any martial arts library.

HAPKIDO II
By Dr. He-young Kimm.
This book is a great resource of information for the Hapkido Practitioner. Each technique is broken down into twelve steps, each pictured for great clarity. A huge work at well over 800 pages, but worth its price.

Traditions
By Dave Lowery.
This is an insightful book into the many obscure traditions of the martial arts and where they come from. Divided into "stand alone chapters", it makes for an easy read. Truly a great book. (One of this author's favorite works).

United States Judo Association Coach Education Manual Level 1
Written by Chris Dewey, P.Hd.
A great work on how to actually teach martial arts, and how learning takes place. A must have for those serious about disseminating the information they have gathered in years of training to their students.

United States Judo Association Coach Education Manual Level 2 and 3

By Dr. Chris Dewey.
Covers things such as conditions of fitness, curriculum building, communication skills, team building, long-range development, personal development, ancillary training, nutrition, and injuries. A great work.

The Art of War
Sun Tzu. Classic.

Ranger Handbook
SH 21-76 Unites States Army. For the serious student of strategy and tactics.

APPENDIX C

THE BIBLE MINISTRY

LIBRARY

The following is a list a books recommended to give you all you will need to have adequate study materials for Bible study, message preparation, and devotion preparation.

Top 10 Books for Research and Study:

First Scofield Study Bible (KJV)
> Based on the 1909 edition of the Scofield Reference Bible. Includes "Righty Dividing the Word of Truth". Oxford Press.

SwordSearcher Bible Software
> Search the Internet for a free downloadable trial version. This is a useful study tool and devotion preparation tool. You can buy the download over the Internet, or order the CD. It is worth the money.

The Great Doctrines of the Bible
> By William Evans. This is a clearly outlined, well-organized, and comprehensive examination of the ten major doctrines of the Christian faith.

Halley's Bible Handbook
> An abbreviated Bible commentary, including information on archaeological discoveries, how we got our Bible, and a short church history.

Strong's Concordance of the Bible
> By James Strong. Every word of the KJV is listed alphabetically, with numbered references to the Greek and Hebrew lexicons.

Bible Version Manual
> Clark. Addresses the topic of which English Bible is the most accurate translation of the manuscripts.

Gipp's Understandable History of the Bible (2nd Edition)
> By Samuel C. Gipp, T.Hd. The history of the Bible and its manuscript evidence written in a clear and understandable manner.

Boyd's Bible Dictionary
> Thousands of Biblical references. Lists and identifies all proper names in the Bible, and provides information on places and events. Complete with pronunciations, definitions, and textual references.

How to Bring Men to Christ

By R.A. Torrey. This helpful book was written for all who are on fire with desire to win people to Christ but simply do not know how. In simple language, Torrey explains how and where to begin and what Scriptures hold the key for particular people in specific situations.

Fast Facts on False Teachings

By Ron Carlson and Ed Decker. This is an all-in-one volume designed to give you some clear facts, instantly. Two world-renown authorities on the cults have combined their extensive knowledge to give you quick, clear facts about today's major cults, false teachings, and false religions, including Atheism, Buddhism, Evolution, the Unification Church, Satanism, and others.

Top 10 Books for Personal Growth:

The Kneeling Christian,

Author Unknown. Answers "How shall I pray? What is prayer? Must I agonize? Does God always answer prayer? Who may pray"?

Morning and Evening

Charles Spurgeon's classic daily devotional.

The Complete Works of E.M. Bounds on Prayer

By E.M. Bounds. Making prayer a key factor in your life develops a closer relationship with the Lord and a greater understanding of His Word. This is what this book is all about.

Why Revival Tarries

By Leonard Ravenhill. This book is meant not only to prevent a decline in spiritual health with the church, but also to encourage a single-minded concern within individuals and groups.

The Pilgrim's Progress.

By John Bunyan. This is a timeless classic of English literature and is an allegory of the Christian's walk with God.

Last Words of Saints and Sinners

By Herbert Lockyer. The author records the dying words of kings, presidents, infidels, martyrs, poets, soldiers, orators, and many others.

A Tale of Three Kings
By Gene Edwards

One Book Stands Alone

By Doug Stauffer

One Book Rightly Divided
By Doug Stauffer

Grace Purpose Giving
By Hugh Taylor

Top 10 Books for Help with your Devotions for Class:

Knight's Master Book of 4,000 Illustrations
By Walter B. Knight. Material topically arranged to make illustrations to drive home Bible teachings easy to find.

Strange Short Stories by the Doctor
By Walter L. Wilson. This is a collection of fascinating lessons for Christians from common, everyday things.

Now You Are Somebody New!
By Hugh Pyle. This is a little booklet for children who have just become Christians. It is designed to help them grow in Christ. It is illustrated, and is a great follow up tool for kids that have accepted Christ.

One Thousand Bible Study Outlines
By F.E. Marsh. This will help the inexperienced Instructor prepare to teach the Word of God. These are easy to use topical briefs.

Vest Pocket Companion for Christian Workers
By R.A. Torrey. This is to help you will souls. The best texts for personal witnessing work classified for practical use. It is printed in full and arranged for ready reference.

The Bible Promise Book
What ever the need of the moment, the answer is to be found in Scripture. This collection of Bible verses is meant for use as a handy reference when you feel the need for the Bible's guidance on a particular problem.

Basics for Believers
By Timothy P. Rose. This series of studies can be used to help strengthen and grow new converts in your class. It will give the specific instructions needed for the new convert to take his very first steps in the Christian walk. It is a book of lessons to help you answer their questions.

Victorious Christians
> By Warren Wiersbe. This is a book of short biographies of Christians of the past, including Luther, Crosby, Taylor, Havergal, and others. Incorporating their life stories into your devotions brings life to the lessons.

A Sure Foundation
> By James W. Knox

About My Father's Business
> By Mark Lawless and Daryl Covington

APPENDIX D:

CONTRIBUTED ESSAYS

CONTRIBUTED ESSAY 1: THE IMPORTANCE OF INTEGRITY

By Michael Mason

In teaching the martial arts one of the most important things is that we realize our position in the hearts and lives of our students. As martial artists and as martial arts instructors, people look at us differently then they do other people. They expect certain things from us that are sometimes very difficult. A martial artist (especially one that is teaching) has to be the example, the model citizen. We have to show with our daily lives that we are more then the average person. We have to show that we will always stand for what is right, even if it is the hardest thing to do.

By always standing up for what is right and true, we show integrity. Now, off hand it may not seem that important to some that the instructor maintain high integrity. Some may wonder what integrity really is. How do you define and abstract concept and how is it that people can have a sense of what integrity is?

To truly understand what integrity is, maybe we should start off with its very definition. According to Webster's New World Dictionary: Third College Edition, the word integrity means:

"1. The quality or state of being complete; unbroken condition; wholeness; entirety 2. the quality or state of being unimpaired; perfect condition; soundness 3. the quality or state of be of sound moral principle; uprightness, honesty, and sincerity."

From this definition, we can see that the third definition is the most appropriate as we look at the concepts of how a martial artist should be perceived, and how they should act. Let's go ahead and take this definition apart in order to gain a further understanding of just what these things are.

The quality or state of being of sound moral principle: What exactly does this mean? What does it mean to have sound moral principles? When we talk about a person's moral principles, we are talking about their ability to determine right from wrong. To state that one must have sound moral principle is to state that they must have the ability to determine right from wrong in their thoughts, words and actions. For example, say that someone tells you a lie. While the lie itself is dishonest, the fact that they felt it okay to tell you the lie is showing low morel principle's. It shows that they were unable to determine that lying is wrong. Moral principles are not the words or actions themselves, but the thought or value behind those words and actions. Moral's are very abstract and therefore require an understanding beyond just "common since".

Uprightness: Once again, this is a definition that can be a little tricky. Uprightness is basically being true to what you stand for. It is being honest, just and honorable. An upright person is someone you know you can go to when you are in a dispute, because they will get both sides, tell the truth and in the end will make a decision that is fair. It is the person you know you can trust. For example, say John never pays you back when he borrows money, but Sally always does. John may ask to borrow $10.00 and you say no, but Sally may ask to borrow $100.00 and you hand it to her with no concern. In this example, John is not very upright because he does not pay you back, but Sally on the other hand is very upright, to the point where you will gladly lend her more then you would John because you know you will get it back. A final definition to this would be honorable. This is a term that in the martial arts we all too often take for granted. An honorable person will always do the right thing, whether this be recovering from a mistake, or simply standing up for what is right. This is similar to when two people have children together, but then split up. The parent that does not have the children should pay child support; it is the right thing to do. Many people (even martial artists) do their best to avoid doing this, which is very dishonorable. Although the situation may not be what we prefer and although it may not be easy, the honorable thing to do is to observe and take care of our responsibilities.

Honesty: This one is fairly self-explanatory. Honesty means to tell the truth. This however is two-fold. Many people understand the concept of being honest with others, but we can only be as honest with others as we are to ourselves. As martial arts instructor's, this is something we NEED to be very concerned with. By being honest with ourselves we help our students learn better martial arts. A common dishonesty among many martial artists today is that their martial art cannot be defeated and is the superior martial art. In reality, all martial arts have their strong and weak points. This dishonesty that many martial artists have with themselves goes from them to their students. In this one act, they are being dishonest with themselves and their students.

Sincerity: Sincerity is something that we see very little of in this day and age. Sincerity is meaning what we say. It means to believe in what we believe in. Many times in the church we see a lack of sincerity. We see people who talk about loving all people and how we are all equal in Gods eyes, and then talk down about the others behind their backs. These are the people we call "fare whether friends". The people who are your friends during good times, but not during bad times. There friendship is not sincere; it is only when it is good for them or makes them look good. We as martial arts instructors must be sincere in our desire to teach our students. When we loose sincerity, we begin not teaching things we need to, letting mistakes go by uncorrected and not teaching for the right reasons. We see this a lot as well in the martial arts world as many instructors teach just for the money, and then you have others who are sincere about helping their students and therefore oftentimes teach for little to no money.

You may be wondering about this time why these things and the different aspects of integrity are being included in a book about teaching the martial arts. The name of this book gives a very good clue; "Teaching the Warrior's Heart". The heart of the martial artists must be pure, true, honest, honorable and sincere. They must always remember their place in the lives of their students and their place in the community. When a martial arts instructor fails in his/her integrity, they do not just affect themselves, but also their students.

In order for a martial arts instructor to be able to truly teach their students, the students need to trust the instructor. This is the first place that integrity comes in. If the instructor is lacking in their integrity, then how are the students to trust him/her? The instructor-student relationship has always been a strong bond and one that should last for a lifetime, but if there is no integrity, the best that can be hoped for are a few that will stay for a few years. If we lack integrity, then we are not only being dishonest with ourselves, but also with our students. We begin to do things that people are unable to agree with on the most basic levels and begin endorsing concepts of action that are less then honorable. In the movie Karate Kid, the mean Sensei teaching at the dojo lacks integrity. His actions are not honorable, and he is prone to be very dishonest. He is dishonest with his students and teaches them to do the wrong things, and he is dishonest with himself as to his true ability (as is shown in the end against Mr. Miyagi). By the end of the movie, his lack of integrity brings his entire school down. In the next movie, we see that he has lost all of his students and has to close his dojo. What caused this downfall of a once large school? Lack on integrity on the part of the instructor.

In the martial arts world we tend to like talking about philosophies and wisdom. Within these things, as an essential element, is integrity. As martial arts instructors, it is our job to teach our students about philosophy and to help them grow, not only in the physical techniques of the martial arts, but also in their spiritual understanding. It is our job to help them understand the values that are held dear in the martial arts. In order for us to be able to teach them, we must first understand them ourselves. What we don't understand, our students will have to fight with on their own. If they are having to do it on their own, then what are we teaching them?

There are two very defined aspects to the martial arts. These are the martial aspect and the art aspect. At most all martial arts schools we will see the martial aspect being taught. Students learning to punch, kick, block, throw, trap and grapple. But let's not forget the other aspect; let's not forget to teach the art of our martial arts. The best way to teach something so abstract is by example, and the first example should be that of integrity. Once our integrity is established, our students will open their minds to learning all about courtesy, perseverance, self-control and indomitable spirit. They will open their minds to what we have to say, because we will have commanded their respect, not just demanded it.

CONTRIBUTED ESSAY 2: 10 WAYS TO RAISE A STREET SMART CHILD
By Fariborz Ashakh

Teachers across the nation have implemented programs boasting claims such as "Mug Proof Your Child", "Ultimate Kids Self-defense" and other self-proclaiming titles. As a martial artist dedicated to teaching kids and adults true self-defense, I have spent years researching these "self-defense programs". Much of what is being taught in the way of self-defense in the United States is bogus; in reality, it just won't work, especially with children.

Bruce Lee's character in the film, Enter The Dragon, when asked his style, replied, "It is the art of fighting without fighting". The bully of the movie wanted to see it. We all remember the scene; Bruce forced the guy into a small lifeboat (a Chinese Junk) to supposedly go over to an island and fight. When the guy got in, Bruce pushed him out to sea. This classic moment in the movie is the concept behind teaching kids to be street smart.

Below are 10 ideals to implement in your teaching of children. Not only can you help the children, but the adults as well. A "clinic" for parents may be a great way to use these concepts to help kids:

1. GIVE KIDS PERMISSION TO SAY NO TO ADULTS
This gives the program its strong foundation. It is important for children to have the support of their parents and to realize they have ownership of their bodies and minds. There should be no forced affection. Let them know that they have rights just like adults. Remember what it felt like to have to kiss people you did not want to? It's fake! If a child learns from their parents that they should kiss someone they do not want to kiss, then they begin to get confused about the proper limits of affection. If the situation arises when another adult tells the child to kiss or touch them, it makes it harder for a child to say no. In your own life, make sure you honor kids. Ask them if you can have a hug or a kiss, rather than telling them or just physically grabbing them. Make it their choice – their decision. The

better that they get at making decisions, the better chance they will make the right one when Mom and Dad are not around and they are responsible for themselves.

2. NO SHORTCUTS

Any time a child takes a different route home, he or she is running the risk of being grabbed with no witnesses. The techniques we teach for children to defend themselves against adults mainly focus upon denying abductors privacy, drawing public attention to the situation, and deriving help from other adults. Make sure kids know that if they are ever grabbed, they must yell and scream "Help, you are not my mom!" or "You are not my dad!" This will elicit a much more powerful response than just a call for help. Therefore, children shouldn't take shortcuts through the woods, backyards or side streets where abductions could occur with no witnesses. Encourage kids to take the same route home each day. This will help friends or parents find them if they are late. And develop safe zones with neighbors. A community needs to help protect its children.

3. IMPORTANT INFORMATION

All children should memorize their name, address and phone number. Parents' names and work numbers are also valuable information to have. This is extremely important in order for kids to be able to tell the police, or other helpful adults how to get in touch with their parents. Make sure children know their area code as well, in case they are abducted and are able to escape to call home themselves. Teach specific drills for dialing 911 and 0 so that the kids know what to do in case of an emergency at home. Let them know how serious it is, and that it is only for emergencies. All children should memorize their name, address and phone number. Parents' names and work numbers are also valuable information to have.

4. WHEN LOST

We all remember a time in our childhood when we got lost and were terrified. We have also all seen children screaming or crying in stores or witnessed panicked parents trying to locate lost children. Having a prearranged course of action should this situation ever occur is a wise strategy. If a child gets lost, teach them to go to the front of the store and tell someone at the register or a policeman to please call for their parents. Remaining calm is an important issue here. It gives kids confidence to know exactly what to do. Tell them to look for people in uniform such as a policeman or a cashier at a store. If you are in a store and you've lost one of your children, do not leave the store – wait at the counter or contact the Lost & Found Department.

5. TRUST YOUR INSTINCTS

For instance, if a child tells you that a certain person gives them a bad feeling and makes them uncomfortable, believe them. If they feel that they are being followed or someone is trying to get them, teach them to go in the opposite direction. Make sure kids know they are never to speak to strangers especially passers by in cars. They can be grabbed too quickly. If they can hear the person, they are too close to the car. Teach children to ignore people they don't know who try to talk to them. Teach them if they think they are being followed, to go to a neighbor's house or into a store. If someone tries to talk to them or grab them, teach them to run in the opposite direction. If a car slows down or if a person in a car asks for directions, teach them to stay away from the car. Make sure that you and all your instructors understand how important it is to tell kids that it is not rude to ignore people they do not know.

6. CHECK IT OUT

All parents lead busy, hectic lives – kids, school, jobs, and social lives. Do you know how many people I have had interview me and ask me what my qualifications were as an instructor? Or ask if I had ever been in trouble with the law and checked out my references? Only 3 in my 12-year teaching career! That's ridiculous! Parents can never know enough about those people who have responsibility for their children. This includes teachers, baby-sitters, coaches, preachers, other friends' parents, anyone. Check into their backgrounds; their last job, references, police record and see how you feel about them personally. Do not trust a referral. Never let someone do your job for you. Do it yourself and do it thoroughly.

7. CODE WORD

This is VITAL! Make sure that parents and kids select a confidential code word. Maybe it's not convenient, but it is life saving. Most abductions are by familiar faces – friends, co-workers, even relatives. Teach parents to decide with their kids on a secret word that only the parent and the child know; something fun and silly like pizza, lipstick, Domon (a Gundum character) and tell them to make sure it's something unique. Make sure that parents leave a list of people that their child is allowed to go home with at school or at a friend's house with specific instructions not to release the child to anyone else. Teach children that anyone who comes to pick them up must have this code word. If a person does not know the code word, the child must never go with that person. No code word – don't go – no excuses. The child should not speak to that person anymore if they do not know it. Abductors will make up any excuse, "Your mom is in the hospital. Hurry let's go." Remember, no code word – no ride or talking- even if you know the person.

8. CHERISH YOUR CHILDREN

It is amazing to me that we have to mention this, but many parents and teachers do not realize children are like a blank computer disks. All they really need is love and acceptance from us. Kids are perfect when they are born. All we can do with them is enhance their natural talents and make sure they stay safe. If we were to cherish and love them the way we should, many pedophiles wouldn't even exist. Being loved and nurtured as children, they wouldn't be acting out that victim cycle. Abductors look for lonely kids at a playground or at a school. The ones who are the easiest victims usually get chosen. Let your kids feel totally loved all the time. Help them to be active and never needy for attention or affection.

9. NO PERSONALIZED CLOTHING

I recently took my son to his first day of school. He was the only one in the class of 28 without a personalized book bag, jacket or some other item. When kids get approached, the pervert is looking for anything – a game they are playing, a name that they can use to develop rapport. Remember every person's favorite sound is his own name. That is why we use it so many times in class each day. Recognition and familiarity. If a child's name is called out, they may immediately let their guard down and start talking. Do not teach them to say, "I can't talk to strangers"; teach them Not to speak to strangers. Do not allow them to get caught up in a web of conversation. They are as good as gone if they start talking and get into a conversation. It develops a bond and also puts them within earshot. Some perverts may start whispering to a child, requiring the child to come closer so they can hear. That's when they can get grabbed. Remember, NO NAMES on anything.

10. GOOD TOUCH – BAD TOUCH

This is a sensitive subject to discuss, but it gets very easy with repetition. The parents should teach this lesson. If a child gets used to talking about this, it will then be much easier to report if it ever does occur. Identify that a good touch is a hug, a kiss on the cheek, a pat on the back or shaking hands. "Doesn't it make you feel good when Mom gives you a hug or a kiss"? That feeling is called "good touch". "Bad touch" is if anyone touches their private areas where their "bathing suit covers". Bad touch is also feeling that the touch is "creepy". Let them know if it happens that it isn't their fault and they should tell the teacher, Mom or Dad, or any other adult that they trust. Overcome the stigma of talking about this subject. Let the children know that they can tell Mom, Dad or teacher if someone is "bad touching" them. Believe them and investigate. Discuss the situation with the child. Do not ignore the situation. Help them to know they can trust you and if such a thing happens to them, they are not at fault. This is an important step to the healing process. In most cases, kids are not capable of sexual fantasy. In order to create these images, most kids would have had to be exposed to some sort of pornography or have been abused.

I AM A TEACHER
By Fariborz Ashakh

I am a teacher.

I was born the first moment that a question leaped from the mouth of a child.

I have been many people in many places.

I am Socrates exciting the youth of Athens to discover new ideas through the use of questions.

I am Anne Sullivan tapping out the secrets of the universe into the outstretched hand of Helen Keller.

I am Aesop and Hans Christian Anderson revealing truth through countless stories.

I am Marva Collins fighting for every child's right to an education.

I am Mary McCloud Bethune building a great college for my people, using orange crates for desks.

And I am Bel Kauffman struggling to go Up The Down Staircase.

The names of those who have practiced my profession ring like a hall of fame for humanity.... I am also those whose names and faces have long been forgotten but whose lessons and character will always be remembered in the accomplishments of their students.

I have wept for joy at the weddings of former students, laughed with glee at the birth of their children and stood with head bowed in grief, confused by graves dug too soon for bodies far too young.

Throughout the course of a day I have been called upon to be an actor, friend, nurse and doctor, coach, finder of lost articles, money lender, taxi driver, psychologist, substitute parent, salesman, politician and a keeper of the faith.

Despite the maps, charts, formulas, verbs, stories and books, I have really had nothing to teach, for my students really have only themselves to learn, and I know it takes the whole world to tell you who you are.

I am a paradox.

I speak loudest when I listen the most.

My greatest gifts are in what I am willing to appreciatively receive from my students.

Material wealth is not one of my goals, but I am a full-time treasure seeker in my quest for new opportunities for my students to use their talents and in my constant search for those talents that sometimes lie buried in self- defeat.

I am the most fortunate of all who labor.

A doctor is allowed to usher life into the world in one magic moment.

I am allowed to see that life is reborn each day with new questions, ideas and friendships.

An architect knows that if he builds with care, his structure may stand for centuries. A teacher knows that if he builds with love and truth, what he builds will last forever.

I am a warrior, daily doing battle against peer pressure, negativity, fear, conformity, prejudice, ignorance and apathy.

But I have great allies: Intelligence, Curiosity, Parental Support, Individuality, Creativity, Faith, Love and Laughter all rush to my banner with indomitable support.

And whom do I have to thank for this wonderful life I am so fortunate to experience, but you the public, the parents.

For you have done me the greatest honor to entrust your greatest contribution to eternity, your children.

And so I have a past that is rich in memories.

I have a present that is challenging adventurous and fun because I am allowed to spend my days with the future.

I am a teacher...and I thank God every day.

CONTRIBUTED ESSAY 3: CAN A CHRISTIAN STUDY AIKIDO
By Mark Barlow

I was raised in a staunch Southern Baptist home and during my 30 years of training, I've heard the same negative opinions and attitudes that have concerned you. When I started Judo as a teen, I was warned that martial arts required bowing to false idols. Not true. When I expanded my training to Jujitsu and Aikido, I was told that they would require meditation which opened the door to a weakening of my faith and attacks on the spirit. Also not true. Meditation turned out to be breathing exercises which allowed me to focus my energy on all aspects of life, not just the martial arts. There are a few (very few, in my experience) schools and instructors that try to interject an element of mysticism or a mishmash of Zen beliefs but while these schools may briefly flourish, they all eventually wither on the vine.

Ki is not magic. It is a heightened awareness of balance and timing combined with proper breathing. Put these together with years of training and you'll be able to achieve superior technique. I've never met a Japanese who proclaimed Ki to be anything spiritual or even particularly special, just a product of practicing basics for years on end. No one looks at a professional athlete and thinks that his ability comes from anything but a natural God given physical talent and the willingness to sweat and bleed until he makes the game look easy. It is the same with martial artist. Whenever someone expresses appreciation for some technique I demonstrate, my response tends to be, "Any 5 year old can do it with 20 years of practice."

The willfully ignorant often condemn that of which they have no personal experience or knowledge. If half the energy that was expended against innocent endeavors would be spent on the sick and needy, we'd be living in a paradise on earth. For every person pointing a finger at the martial arts as ungodly or unchristian, there are a thousand martial artists and instructors living Christian lives and working to help and aid those around them. My sensei was capable of performing many of the ki demonstrations you've probably heard of and I've never met a better, more Christian soul. I'm a better man for having trained with him for 20 years, as are the thousands of lives he touched during the 40 years he taught.

Belief and faith are deeply personal issues. My training has been as a warrior, not a fighter. I train to combat evil and to protect not only myself, but also my loved ones and those around me. As hokey as that sounds, it's how I truly view my involvement with martial arts. My spirit is strong because I devote my physical energies, thought and will to a pure cause and I'm able to be a better husband, worker, student and teacher because of that focus. Any activity can be spiritual whether it's martial arts, knitting or golf. The importance is not in the activity; it's in the intent of the participant. Study aikido, take up biking or collect stamps...doesn't matter. What matters most is the destination, not the journey.

I hope me jumping on my personal soapbox helped.

CONTRIBUTED ESSAY 4: WHEN TRAINING BECOMES REAL LIFE

by Steven Riggs

In recent years we have witnessed thru the news media that young children and teenage girls have come under concentrated attack. Whether the number of attacks have grown or the media has done a better job of highlighting the danger is difficult to determine.

To highlight a few examples we need only to look back thru past newspapers or news broadcasts. Several summers ago a young lady named Elizabeth Smart was kidnapped right out of her bedroom with her younger sister being present and observant at the time. Later in CA there were two young girls on a date that were attacked, boyfriends were tied up, and the girls abducted and held. The two girls attacked and resisted their abductor unsuccessfully but the local police intervened and shot to death the kidnapper to save the teens lives.

In the same general time frame two or three young children between the ages of 4 & 6 were playing near their home. A man came along and asked for help in finding his puppy. It was reported that the girl responded to help and then changed her mind, causing the assailant to grab her and drive off. The young girl was later found dead. In late 2003 a 13 year old girl left her friends house to walk home. This was in a good neighborhood, 4:00 in the afternoon with people in the neighborhood. The teen walked by a car wash with men working and a security camera recording the events. The camera later showed a man in his mid to late 30's dressed in work clothes walk up to her on the sidewalk, gently grasp her elbow and walk her away. She was later found to have been sexually assaulted and murdered.

There are many similarities between these and other cases. Children naturally trust adults, particularly if the adult is in the same age range of a trusted figure such as their own parents or grandparents. Children are remarkably compliant if suddenly ordered to take a certain action or are threatened not to take any action under the duress of violent retribution upon themselves or even on a member of the child's family. As Christian martial arts instructors we must somehow come up with training methods to combat these growing assaults which most often end in sexual assault and death.

I believe there should be several approaches and this article is not meant to infer that these are the only good methods. I believe that teaching what is right and wrong in a supportive role to the parent is paramount. Often our students look up to us and respect us for the part we play in their lives. We should take advantage of that respect and trust by imparting what may be life saving information. We should talk with the parents and be on the same page of the hymn book in giving instructions about how to deal with strangers.

Many parents have already dealt with this issue and have tried many different methods including giving of code words and other methods. I believe that there is a break somewhere between childhood and after puberty where the child begins to develop a greater ability to think rationally and logically about a new and potentially dangerous situation as it presents itself. Young children can not do that as much as we may wish that they could. I have changed my entire teaching method for my younger students to take that into account. In every case I have had full parental support.

What I am about to share may seem radical to some but I believe it is necessary in the world in which we live. Our society is a dangerous one from a practical level of violent people being released from prison all over America each and every day of the week. From the Bible we know all this to be true with the added warning that this will only get worse as time goes on.

I believe that most 16 year olds on up can probably logically access the potential danger to themselves and make the effort to resist either being in the wrong place at the wrong time or what to do if they are. Young children can not do that and we must acknowledge that. I work with my young students both boys and girls in a very strict and direct way of defense against adults. FBI statistics show that 1 in every 3 women in America will be sexually assaulted in their lifetime. For men it is 1 in 6, so our instructions need to be for both boys and girls.

In our classes we teach the children to avoid contact with any strange adults when outside of their parents presence. For those that think I am harsh or to reactionary, I acknowledge your right to disagree but my total concern is with my student's welfare. One of my greatest fears is visiting one of my students in the hospital or at the funeral because I didn't do my job well enough. We teach our young children to react immediately without thought to any stranger putting their hand or attempting to put their hand upon them.

Adults can be subtle and try to shake their hands under the pretense of grabbing them or offering candy. Our training teaches that the moment a stranger approaches to touch them, they 1st scream, 2nd run and 3rd strike as many violent techniques at the adult as they are capable of doing. I do not teach a 10 year old 75lb girl to use a reverse punch to an adults face. Rather we teach a palm heel or jab to the groin, a thumb in the eye, biting the closest body part, stomping on the foot and clawing at the face and aiming for the larynx in an attempt to crush their windpipe. Some might say this is to violent. I have never had a parent tell me that they felt this way but rather they supported me 100% and encouraged their children to practice as I instructed. (Not however on their brothers or sisters, only in class)..

I used to be a police officer and know a little about the law in my state of North Carolina. I can almost guarantee you that in my area of the state there is no way you could gather a jury of 12 people to side with a stranger who put his hands on a child and, as a result, suffered a terrible trauma such as blindness. If you are an adult just putting your hand upon a child is in itself an assault even if it does no damage. No adult ever,ever,ever, has the right to touch a child without the parents permission.

One of the training methods we have used on a number of occasions is to put the child in a scenario situation where they don't know what is coming and then act out any number of real life encounters. We first discovered that while the students were willing to use their martial arts skills they were slow to respond verbally with calls for help. We have had to increase our repetitiveness on that part of the training. On the positive side of the picture we have had to have adults with padding and a mind set, to be ready to duck as soon as the exercise gets rolling.

One night I had to be away from class and I had an assistant instructor with one of my top students who also has four of his own children in the program. The next day I asked in particular how the reality training sequence of the class went. My student informed me that it went quite well except several adults had been injured during the training. I called that a successful night and the adults who helped out didn't mind a few black and blue marks and scratches.

I cannot emphasize to strongly that the training must be realistic, forceful, even violent if that is the way you want to critique it. I stand behind it because I know it works. I was fortunate to have a two week block of phys. Ed class at a local private Christian school. Some of the younger teens were with me every day for about 9 days straight for well over an hour of training.

On the last day of class I was told that a 14 year old girl had been attacked the previous evening. The teen was with her mother while going to a grocery store. They were separated for a short time as the young lady walked toward the Chinese Restaurant next door. She was suddenly attacked by a man described as being of medium build, 22-26 years of age with no remarkable features. He put a bear hug on her from behind pinning her arms and lifted her off the ground. She first attempted to break his thumb or finger and failed to break his grip due to the difference in size as he was much older, stronger and heavier. She then arched her back and threw a kick backwards and up into his groin causing him to drop her. As she landed on the ground she executed a front snap kick straight up into his face while he was still bent over. He then ran off and she ran for help and the police were called.

There was not a good description of the man, no license plate readable on his car or anything else to assist the police but one small item. He bled on her shirt. Television has taught us what DNA evidence can do to send people to prison. If and when a suspect is ever caught they have irrefutable evidence of his attack upon her. She suffered a bruise on her hip and the confiscation of a favorite shirt by the police. My point is that she reacted rather than freezing or thinking thru her options. We will never know whether the intent was rape, kidnapping or murder. What we do know is that a bright, young girl who loves the Lord is still with her parents and friends as she should be.

The scriptures make it abundantly clear that we live in a world dominated by evil. There are sinful and violent people all around us at any given moment and we don't who they are. We must be prepared and prepare our students to the reality of how to deal with such a situation.

Hopefully I will never have another student attacked as long as I teach. I would be remiss in thinking that the possibility is not there and not pursue realistic training methods to send them out with. There are teachers in my area that have students who can show off many gold trophies for tournaments won. That is not wrong but I am more concerned that my students survive any type of assault. I cannot make them invulnerable but I can make every effort to give them the physical tools, the mental conditioning and emotional ability to deal with a violent attack.

CONTRIBUTED ESSAY 5: GET UP!!
By Joseph Lumpkin

As we study the Old Testament, we find it teaches of our need for a savior. The Old Testament promises His coming. The New Testament proclaims His life, death, resurrection, and imminent return. We see and understand our need for a savior. Yet, in our study we often skim over those few scriptures containing His ministry and words. Out a volume containing 66 books, there are only four short books that contain His life. Most of those small works repeat one another. So often we overlook the very seed and core of our faith; those books of His life, His ministry, and His sayings. What was Jesus trying to tell us?

Certainly He was telling us we need Him and should accept Him as Savior and Lord. We know He came and died, as payment for our sins, but there is more. Jesus also told us how to treat each other and how to live our lives. This message we must shout from the rooftops. With this message we cannot be silent. To the woman caught in adultery, He did not condemn her but gave her another chance. He said, "GET UP". To the daughter who had died, leaving her father no hope, he gave hope. He said, "GET UP". To Lazarus, his best friend, who lay in the grave three days and was completely without life, He gave life. He said, "GET UP!" To Paul, who was knocked down, beaten, thrown in jail, and held in prison, He gave courage to go on. He said, "GET UP". To Jesus who lay dead in a tomb, the Father in Heaven gave Lordship! He said "GET UP". And when He comes for me, I may be dead, working in the field, laboring on the rooftop, sweating in the mill, or asleep in my bed, but the words will be the same. With the sound of a trumpet, with the voice of an archangel, we who believe will all hear Him say, "GET UP, GET UP, GET UP! You cannot win unless you keep getting up. You cannot be victorious in the battle unless you keep getting up. We will all fall, but he said "GET UP". We will all fail but we must GET UP.

The world is not our friend. It would see faith in God fail, but we must keep getting up! We fight an enemy who wants to knock us down, keep us down, and see us ruined. But Paul said, I may be knocked down but I am not out! Paul proclaimed we were to finish the race. He got back up! Solomon said, Here is a righteous man, a man who although he falls seven times, he keeps getting up! Jesus said to those caught in sin, "GET UP"! To those who have sorrow, "GET UP"! To those who have lost all hope, "GET UP"! The only way to fail is not to get up. YOU MUST GET UP! He will be there when the race is over. He will meet us when our battle is through. GET UP! It is time for Christians to unite. Tell those you love to GET UP; help those in need to GET UP; Strengthen those who have fallen and HELP LIFT THEM. Tell them to GET UP. Do not punish, do not judge, do not condemn. Our fight is with Satan and those who would keep us down. Our fight is with the world, not with each other. Though the world hates us, politicians loathe us, friends forsake us, judges won't let us pray, laws are made against our will, government steals our land, our money and our rights; through we are tested with sickness, debt, and despair, GET UP! It is not over GET UP! He is coming soon. GET UP! GET UP! GET UP! And teach your children to keep GETTING UP!

If you want to know why we train in martial arts, if you wonder why we worship God, if you are puzzled as to why we fight against our limitations; it is to have the strength in our spirits and the will of mind to keep getting up until Jesus comes again.

APPENDIX E:

TECHNIQUES AND TIPS

TO KEEP YOUR CLASS

FROM GETTING STALE

We are what we repeatedly do; excellence then is not an act, but a habit. – Aristotle

Time and time again martial arts instructors ask, "What do you do to keep the class fresh?" One of the best ways to keep students interested in class, and to keep their energy level high, is to train hard on your own. Practice your techniques diligently, but beyond that; focus your training on acquiring more knowledge of the techniques you already know. A good martial art teacher needs to learn about anatomy and kinesiology, the history and philosophy of martial art, and the psychology, sociology and methodology of teaching.

Another thing to add to the class is variety. If you always do the same thing over and over, it gets old. Repetition is the key to perfecting techniques, but sometimes it is boring. Can you remember standing in "niunja ja sae" T-stance for an hour, week after week, kicking the same old "ap cha kee" (front kick) over and over and over? So what is the secret? Disguise the repetitions. Do some line drills, some focus pad drills, some kicking shield drills, and some bag work. Mix it up. Here are some ideals to disguise repetition:

1. The Wave: Have the whole class get in a circle. You start a technique. As soon as you do the technique, the person to your right does it. As soon as he does it, the person to his right does it. This goes on until the technique goes all the way around the circle, like a wave. Continue, and get faster and faster, then stop and go in the other direction.

2. Sensei Says: With younger kids (my adult class loves this game, too) play "Simon Says", but change it to "Sensei Says", and call out martial arts techniques. The last one left will be "Sensei" for the next round.

3. Bull in the Ring: Put one student in the center, and gather the rest of the class around him. Give each student a number. When their number is called, they charge the student in the center and attack with

a predetermined strike, throw, or takedown. The student in the center is to defend by using that same technique. After the student has defended against everyone in the circle, the next student comes in, and the whole process begins again.

In addition to these three drills, the following are some drills and exercises that Erle Montaigue uses for teaching students. I have edited and rewritten some of the descriptions for clarity, but the majority of the concepts and methods are his.

1. Kick Defense: This drill makes use of the legs in defending against an attack. (This fits wonderfully into the Shinsei System since we defend against attacks below the waist with our legs, and defend against kicks by checking them with our feet if at all possible). When practicing this drill, the student should not use their hands but instead concentrate all efforts to the legs and feet. They must use the low kicks to the knees or back kicks to the groin area. The back turning kick is handy here or the back spinning kick, low kicks to the legs is also useful. The students should also be trained on the bag, always using the front leg to kick.

2. 'V' Step Kicking: In the *Shinse Hapkido* system, we would call this, "using our angles of evasion". One person attacks with a front snap kick to the abdomen it could actually be any type of centerline kick. The student must step out to the side with his front leg in a 'V' to avoid the attack while blocking it and re-attacking with his other foot to the knee.

3. Barging: This technique is used against most kicks. As the partner prepares to kick high you have detected his intention and have barged in thus destroying his timing and defeating his attempt to kick. You then continue with that momentum slamming your arms across his chest or face. You may wish to use another appropriate technique such as a elbow strike or takedown also. The primary goal is to detect the attack and barge in, moving before the technique is launched.

4. 8-Kicking: This technique comes from pa-kua Chang and involves the use of the whole lower body to gain power in the most effective

low kicks. The aim is to gain stability while swiveling on the ball of the standing foot and executing an effective kick to the legs.

One person is the kicker the other the defender. The kicker kicks with his left foot to the opponent's legs. You detect it and kick to his knee with your right low heel kick (learned on the bag). He then pulls his foot back and attacks with another low kick with the same foot. You spin on your left toes and execute a back stomp to his oncoming knee. He then kicks low with his right foot. You use 'slap' kick (learned on the bag) to the inside of his knee. He then attacks with his left foot again and you use back low hook kick to damage his calf muscle and nerve points. You then change immediately to the other leg and do the same on the left side, thus the 8-kicking method.

5. 90-Degree Kicking: This involves the student stepping to the side as the kick comes in. He attacks with a strike straight out at 90 degrees from him to gain the most power.

6. Snake Fingers: This technique trains the use of the fingers to attack the opponent's vital points. The fingers should be trained on the mitt so they become strong and one is trained in the 'spring' technique so the fingers will not be hurt.

Your partner throws a left jab. You thrust your right fingers into his eyes, which simultaneously blocks his attack. He attacks again with left jab so you block on the inside with your left fingers turned upward and again slip off to strike the eyes. He attacks again with left jab so you step with your left foot (you started out with your left foot forward) to your right and cross step as you simultaneously block and strike to his eyes with your left fingers.

He attacks with a right jab so you spin around lifting your right foot off the ground and attack as you block with your right fingers to his eyes. He attacks with right jab so you step to your left with your right foot and cross step as you attack to his eyes with your right fingers.

You are now in the opposite position so you can now begin on the other side.

7. Foot Slap: Your partner kicks to your groin. You block it with your foot and attack to his groin. He blocks with his foot and attacks to your groin.

8. Blind Mitt Training: Partner stands holding one mitt. You have your eyes closed. He says 'go' and you open your eyes. You do not look at the mitt but rather use your peripheral vision to see it and attack it with whatever portion is appropriate. Your speed and power must be at a maximum. This can extend to using the feet, head and elbows.
Your partner holds two mitts. You close your eyes. He says 'go' and you open an attack at either mitt. He immediately moves the other mitt, which you must also hit.

9. Using Voice: Your partner stands in front of you and moves to strike you with any technique. You make a sound with your voice to stop the attack. Later you can combine the voice with a point with one palm. This has the effect of making for very fast reaction times, as the voice is a bridge between the physical and the abstract.

10. Distance: This trains you to strike as soon as the opponent is within range. This could mean when any part of his body is within range. You do some sparring and make sure you attack him as soon as he is within your striking range. In this way he should never be able to hit you because you have hit him before he has the chance to strike. You snuff out his feet and hand attacks before they start; or if they have begun, you put his timing way out.

11. Push Mitt: Have your eyes closed as your partner holds a mitt. He pushes you anywhere to put you off balance. You immediately open your eyes and strike the mitt, which could be held anywhere.

12. Shock Value: We can be defeated usually because the 'shock' value of the opponent's attack catches us off guard. If he hits us while we are thinking 'What has happened?' he has already hit again. We use double push hands to train to combat this method. Our partner hits

us with an explosive strike during push hands. We should strike as soon as the attack has happened, thus stopping the second attack. If we do not attack then the partner will attack us again and again.

13. Two Kicks: This is an excellent training method using two bags and two other people. Your partners stand in front of you, one with the bag at knee level to your side, the other with the bag at knee level in front of you. You kick the first bag to the side using a low round kick and immediately bounce off that bag into a back kick onto the other bag.

14. Street Attack: Your partner has all of the protective equipment. He attacks you relentlessly with all of the force that he can find. You must use whatever is appropriate to defend yourself, that is, the closest object, be it head, elbow knee, fist or palm. You must bring him to the ground or he will just keep on coming and attacking you.

KICKING SPEED DRILLS

SPEED KICKS I HOLDER: With 2 paddles, hold paddle in position for 45° kicks (Korean Beet Chagi) KICKER: Single leg 45°kicks (10 each leg); Then alternate 45°kicks (20 total)

SPEED KICKS II HOLDER: Hold paddle in position for 45° kicks (Beet Chagi)< KICKER: Kick paddle once, then twice, then three….until you reach 10 kicks. Put kicking foot back to starting position after each kick. Do as quickly and accurately as possible. Switch legs.

REACTION DRILL
HOLDER: Hold paddle behind your back and quickly move paddle towards front for a 45° kick (Beet Chagi), or roundhouse kick (Dolro Chagi), or ax kick (Nehryuh Jeek Gi), or spin kick (Dwi Dol Yeo Chagi), or back kick (Dwi Chagi). KICKER: Try to anticipate the paddle (an opening in your opponent's defense), but do not kick before paddle comes out.

ENDURANCE DRILLS

TWO MINUTE DRILL HOLDER: With 2 paddles, hold paddle in position for any kick (round house, front snap, back kick, spin kick, ax kick...) and change paddle position after each kick. Try to think ahead and place paddles at probable next kick positions to avoid awkward kicking combination by the kicker. KICKER: Continuously kick the paddles for 2 minutes. Try to make your movements flow and conserve your energy. NOTE: Beginners may want to start out with 30 seconds and work up to 2 minutes.

GERMAN DRILL
Work at 90% of your maximum heart rate, kick midsize pads with double-kicks (pit Chagi) for 10 seconds then rest for 10 seconds, then kick for 10 seconds again. Continue this drill for a total of 2 minutes for beginners, then go to 3 minute founds for intermediate and advanced.

COUNTERS Note: Counters given should be practiced with both legs, not just as the examples below:
Players in OPEN stance: Offensive player kicks with 45° kick (Beet Chagi). Defensive player counters with a turning back kick (Dwi Chagi).
Players in CLOSED stance: Offensive player kicks with back leg right 45° kick (Beet Chagi). Defensive player slide towards opponent with a right punch to chest then left 45° kick to abdomen.
Players in CLOSED stance: Offensive player kicks with back leg right 45° kick (Beet Chagi). Defensive player counters with front leg ax-kick.
Players in OPEN stance: Offensive player kicks with back leg right 45° kick (Beet Chagi). Defensive player slides back then counters with double kick; first kick to the buttocks area to draw opponent's attention (do not use force, this kick is only used to divert his attention) then second kick to opponent's abdomen.

RUNNING DRILLS

ENDURANCE:

Two miles slow jog; sprint at the end of the run. Alternate: slow jog (3 minutes) and sprint (45 seconds). For team practice: Jog in a line around track, the last person sprint to the front of the line, then the next last person.

AGILITY:

Mark a 25-yard track every 5 yards. From starting position, sprint to the 5-yard mark, touch floor (ground), and sprint back to starting position, touch floor (ground), sprint to 10-yard mark, and touch floor (ground).

For Team practice: Line up team in a large circle 3-5 feet apart. The last person runs in and out of the circle. (Go to left, run past one member, then go right, run past another, then left...). Try to have people running continuously, try to have space between you and the person in front of you to avoid stopping.

APPENDIX F:

MINISTRY PROPOSAL

SAMPLE

Depending on the situation, you may be asked by your local church, pastor, or facility director to present a ministry proposal / business proposal. The following is an actual proposal done by Steven Riggs that may serve as an example in your personal drafting, if need be.

AMERICAN DEFENSIVE ARTS ALLIANCE
Christ-centered Martial Arts Training
Ephesians 6:10-12 Philippians 2:3-4

PROPOSAL: To operate a Christ-centered martial arts program committed to inspire, encourage, and equip its students not only to become better martial artists, but more importantly, to become bold effective witnesses for Jesus Christ.

PURPOSE: To use the martial arts as a tool to share God's Truth in a natural way in a non- threatening environment with believers and unbelievers.

GOALS:
1. To provide quality martial arts training in a "Christian" atmosphere for families (Chapel and non-Chapel) who desire martial arts/self-defense training, but do not want exposure to the humanistic and/or Eastern philosophies normally associated with the martial arts.

2. To reach into the community, providing a vehicle for evangelism to people who would either never darken the doors of a church, or who attend a local church and believe they are Christians, but don't truly know Jesus Christ.

3. To aid in the spiritual growth and discipleship of believers (especially teens and children), teaching Truth in a different manner than what they are exposed to elsewhere (Sunday School, Childrens' Church, youth programs, etc.)

METHODS:

1. When & Where: Two class periods per week on Saturday morning and Tuesday evening. Neil Clark Recreation Center would be the preferred location for Saturday morning, possibly operating under HCC's agreement with the City for use of the building. The main room in HCC's worship center would be the site for Tuesday evening (and Saturday morning, if Neil Clark is not available). When the HCC room is used, we would be responsible for taking down and replacing chairs necessary for space, making no extra labor for Jeff Blanchard. (Note: There isa possibility that the Tuesday/Thursday karate class now meeting at Neil Clark will be leaving that location by the- end of 2003. If so, we could hopefully move the program there on Tuesday evening. Eventually, when our new building is complete, we could operate entirely on the HCC campus.

2. Who: Students

a. HCC children, youth, adults and their friends. This offers them (especially the youth) an activity to invite their unsaved friends to where they will be exposed to the gospel and be among Christians in a non-religious setting.

b. Non-HCC chm who desire training in an atmosphere where basic Christian principles are taught and lived-out.

c. The un-churched community who desire quality martial arts training in this setting for whatever reason...lower rates, a sense of safety commonly associated with churches, location, etc.

Who : Instructors

I will be the senior and primary instructor. My rank and experience are outlined on the attached resume. I have been certified as an instructor by the Oriental Defensive Arts Association, Christian Martial Arts Association, and Black Belts of the Faith (BBFI). My certification from BBFI is at level five, which means I have technical expertise, superior understanding of the art form, experience in teaching, and a formal Bible education (Bachelor of Science in Bible/Christian Education from Lancaster Bible College, Lancaster, PA). Assisting in instruction will be Richard Elrod, a 26 year old believer who has attended HCC and been discipled on a limited basis by myself. Richard holds the rank of first degree black belt in Heishin karate and currently assists me in teaching my existing students. As students progress technically and mature spiritually, I hope to have some assist when appropriate, allowing them the opportunity to use their skills and gifts in a more advanced manner.

3. How:
Besides realistic and practical self-defense, students will be learning respect for others as well as themselves, confidence, respect for the martial arts, sound doctrine and scripture. Classes will be more efficient if divided into the age brackets of 6-11 years (K grade) and 12-99 years (middle school-adult). All input and instruction will be at age appropriate levels.

Martial arts instruction will be in Tang Soo Do, a traditional Korean style of karate. The martial arts are frequently abused, but abuse will not be tolerated Students will be taught to consider the information and techniques they learn as to be used for defense purposes ONLY. Students caught abusing the techniques and 4isrespecting the policies and art of our school will be suspended or expelled from class. Safety will be of the utmost importance: free-sparring will be allowed only with proper safety gear; throws will not be taught without mats/cushion surface. Note: In 28 years, I have had one student injured with a broken finger, a much better safety record than basketball, skiing, soccer and many other physical activities.

The martial arts began in and are often surrounded by Eastern mysticism. We will teach that we are to serve only the One Master, our Lord and Savior Jesus Christ. A devotional and time of prayer will be a part of every class. Assuming the classes will consist of both believers and unbelievers, emphasis will be twofold: evangelism and discipleship. We must prepare the soil (build relationships and gain the trust of the students), plant the seeds (share the gospel of salvation), water the seeds (continue to share and build on the foundation laid) and harvest the souls God brings to Himself, while at the same time feeding and discipling those who are already God's children. Wherever applicable, lessons in Truth will be tied in to the activity being taught. While scripture memorization will not be a requirement for achieving rank, a clear understanding of scriptural principles will be tested orally as part of examinations for rank. The Bible will be the principle source of material with some use of material from other sources, as well as input from HCC staff (primarily Matt Parker and Kathy Rhoton). It is my hope and desire that adult volunteers from the Chapel will become involved in the teaching/discipling process, whether or not they themselves are students in the class.

4. Cost:
Voluntary donation/offering. After the first month or so of instruction, each student will be expected to purchase a uniform (gi) for class. Also safety equipment will be necessary for free-sparring. Both these items can be ordered through me at minimal cost.

CONCLUSION:
I look forward to the opportunity to answer any questions. Thank you for prayerfully considering this proposal.
Respectfully submitted,
Steven C. Riggs February 18, 2003

APPENDIX G:

Karate for Christ International

Officers

Daryl Covington, President and CEO
David Dunn, Vice President, International Affairs
Michael Lewis, U.S. Operations President
David Price, U.S. Operations Vice-President
Leslie Sowl, Membership
George Petrotta, Tae Kwon Do
Joseph Lumpkin, Hapkido
Dave Sgro, Tang Soo Do
Erle Montaigue, Chinese and Philippines Arts
Michael Lewis, Japanese Arts
Kang Rhee, Honorary
Karl Marx, American Arts
Jim Carpenter, Tournaments
Jim Payne, Chaplain
Tim Faulk, Missions Executive Director
Bobby Monger, Assistant to the Executive Director
Hugh Taylor, Missions Liaison Advisor

APPENDIX H:

Ranking Board

This service is only offered to our "certified" schools or members.

ALL RANK ISSUED THROUGH THE KARATE FOR CHRIST RANKING
BOARD SHALL BE TESTED FOR. THERE IS NO CROSS RANKING. IN
ADDITION TO EACH STYLE'S REQUIREMENTS FOR RANK, THE
FOLLOWING ARE ADDED FOR ALL STYLES:

I DEGREE
GENERAL REQUIREMENTS
- At least 15 years old.
- A minimum of three years training in the martial arts.
- Must have a personal relationship with Jesus Christ.
- Provide Christian character references from their pastor, teachers, principal, employer, or instructor.
- Must be a member of Karate for Christ International.

II DEGREE
GENERAL REQUIREMENTS
- Must have a personal relationship with Jesus Christ.
- At least 16 years old and a minimum of one year as I Degree.
- A minimum of four years training in the martial arts.
- Has demonstrated the physical, mental, and spiritual maturity worthy of the Christian black belt during the year as I Degree.
- Provide Christian character references from their pastor, teachers, principal, employer, or instructor.
- Must be a member of Karate for Christ International.

III DEGREE
GENERAL REQUIREMENTS
- Must have a personal relationship with Jesus Christ.
- At least 18 years old and a minimum of two years as a II Degree
- A minimum of six years training in the martial arts.
- At least one year as an assistant instructor.

- Provide Christian character references from their pastor, teachers, principal, employer, or instructor
- Must have be a member of Karate for Christ International for at least 1 year.
- Must be currently teaching a class.

IV DEGREE
GENERAL REQUIREMENTS

- Must have a personal relationship with Jesus Christ.
- At least 22 years old and a minimum of three years as a III Degree.
- A minimum of nine years training in the martial arts.
- Provide Christian character references from their pastor, teachers, principal, employer, or instructor
- Must have be a member of Karate for Christ International for at least 1 year.
- Must have been instructing as member school of Karate for Christ International for at least 1 year.
- Must be currently teaching a class.

V DEGREE
GENERAL REQUIREMENTS

- Must have a personal relationship with Jesus Christ.
- At least 30 years old and a minimum of four years as a IV Degree.
- A minimum of fifteen years training in the martial arts.
- Provide Christian character references from their pastor, teachers, principal, employer, or instructor
- Provide three promotion recommendations from three black belts ranking IV Degree, or higher.
- Must have be a member of Karate for Christ International for at least 2 years.
- Must have been instructing as member school of Karate for Christ International for at least 2 years.
- Must be currently teaching a class.

VI DEGREE
GENERAL REQUIREMENTS

- Must have a personal relationship with Jesus Christ.
- At least 35 years old and a minimum of five years as a V Degree.
- A minimum of twenty years training in the martial arts.
- Hold master instructor rank.
- Provide Christian character references from their pastor, teachers, principal, employer, or instructor
- Provide three promotion recommendations from three black belts ranking

IV Degree, or higher
- Must have be a member of Karate for Christ International for at least 2 years.
- Must have been instructing as member school of Karate for Christ International for at least 2 years.
- Must be currently teaching a class.

VII DEGREE
GENERAL REQUIREMENTS
- Must have a personal relationship with Jesus Christ.
- At least 40 years old and minimum of five years as a VI Degree.
- A minimum of twenty-five years training in the martial arts.
- Hold master instructor rank.
- Provide Christian character references from their pastor, teachers, principal, employer, or instructor
- Provide three promotion recommendations from three black belts ranking IV Degree, or higher
- Must have be a member of Karate for Christ International for at least 2 years.
- Must have been instructing as member school of Karate for Christ International for at least 2 years.
- Must be currently teaching a class.

VIII DEGREE
GENERAL REQUIREMENTS
- Must have a personal relationship with Jesus Christ.
- At least 55 years old and a minimum of five years as a VII Degree
- A minimum of thirty-five years training in the martial arts.
- Hold master instructor rank.
- Provide Christian character references from their pastor, teachers, principal, employer, or instructor
- Provide three promotion recommendations from three black belts ranking IV Degree, or higher
- Must have be a member of Karate for Christ International for at least 2 years.?
- Must have been instructing as member school of Karate for Christ International for at least25 years.
- Must be currently teaching a class.

For ranking "Through" Karate for Christ International, Michael Lewis is the point of contact. Email: kfciuskaicho@msn.com

Process for School Certification

- Send Copies of rank certificates for review

- Send video footage of their class and Bible study / and or:

APPENDIX I:

Instructor/School Certification Quiz

This is an open book test 41 questions you need 85% to pass.
Please number a page 1 through 41 type your answers for the questions next to the corresponding numbers. When you finish the test e-mail it to David Dunn Vice President KFCI for grading. daviddunn@mchsi.com

1. A & B
2. D
3. A
Etc.

When your done paste them to a e-mail and send them back. Good Luck!

KFCI Test Questions

1. *Standing Orders* as it applies to a Karate for Christ International Certified Instructor refers to:
   a. Running your school like the United States Army Airborne Division
   b. A plan that you make up to follow with rigid rules and regulations
   c. Using the Karate for Christ Instructor's Certification Manual as a guideline for your ministry and classes
   d. None of the above

2. The guidelines and references to the United States Army mentioned in the Karate for Christ International Instructor's Certification Manual means that you as a certified instructor should:
   a. Be a former member of the United States Army before you can apply as a Karate for Christ School/Instructor
   b. Structure your program based upon the United States Army guidelines
   c. Use these guidelines as a base to outline your own mission and purpose for teaching within the real of Christian martial arts
   d. All of the above

3. Choose the answers that best describe the teachings of the Hwa Rang Warriors and the Code of the Ancient Warrior as it applies to Christian Martial Arts (choose all that apply).
   a. Hwa Rang Warriors were Christians that happened to live in Korea
   b. The Code of the Ancient Warrior can be taught and applied using biblical principles
   c. Instructors of Korean martial arts should instruct and model the Code of the Ancient Warriors because it is a criteria of being a Karate for Christ International Instructor
   d. There are five principles in the Code of the Ancient Warrior
   e. There are nine virtues of the Hwa Rang Warriors
   f. The nine virtues of the Hwa Rang Warriors do not have any place in a Christian martial arts class because they are not biblical principles

4. Using these virtues of the Hwa Rang Warrior and Codes of the Ancient Warrior insures the student understands the purpose behind the martial arts training he is receiving, learns about the Korean culture, and is exposed to Biblical truth.
   a. True
   b. False

5. The Karate for Christ Instructor's Creed is optional as a KFCI Certified Instructor.
   a. True
   b. False

6. Choose any of the following that are part of the Karate for Christ International Instructor's Creed (choose all that apply).
   a. I am patient and enthusiastic
   b. I demand respect of every student
   c. I go the extra mile, always giving more than the expected amount
   d. I never punish, I discipline
   e. I never tell students about their talent to prevent them from having large egos

7. I treat every student I meet like they are the most important people. Why?
   a. Because they are important
   b. We should treat all people with respect
   c. They will give us their friendship and respect in return
   d. All of the above

8. The difference between a martial arts program and a martial arts ministry is:

a. The ministry realizes the greatest thing the children will learn in your class is the Bible

b. There is no difference between a martial arts program and a martial arts ministry

c. Martial arts ministries are free and programs are not

d. A martial arts program is not taught by a Christian instructor

9. Some of the ways to prepare for your weekly devotions in class are:
   a. To copy someone else's lesson plans
   b. Teach the concept you learned at church on Sunday
   c. Prepare all week
   d. Prepare yourself

10. Kang Rhee in his interview stated the following about Christian martial artists:
    a. "A Christian martial artist should be the best person in the world"
    b. "A Christian martial artist should never tell anyone he is a Christian"
    c. "A Christian martial artist is always the best kind of instructor"
    d. Kang Rhee didn't say any of these things

11. Kang Rhee desires that adult students become master:
    a. Students
    b. People
    c. Christians
    d. Workers

12. Kang Rhee states that in the life of a child his/her martial arts instructor:
    a. Is one of the most influential people in that child's life
    b. Is not very important
    c. Cannot take the place of a parent
    d. Is a better influence than the parents of that child

13. Kang Rhee believes that parents should find a martial arts instructor that reflects the values they teach at home and who is a stable example for the child.
    a. True
    b. False

14. The following is from the Pa Sa Ryu Handbook: *The Pa Sa Ryu Martial Artist has a realistic approach to life. He knows that by "trying to chase too many rabbits" he loses his focus and his efforts are in vain. He is self-controlled. He directs his life toward the area, which gives him the most satisfaction and offers opportunity to contribute to society. He has a*

professional attitude and he approaches every challenge with the determination to be the best that he can be.
- a. True
- b. False

15. Your class is a martial arts ministry if you are teaching in a church.
- a. True
- b. False

16. To have a ministry in the bible sense, you must teach the Word as God had kept and preserved it.
- a. True
- b. False

17. The Roman Road is:
- a. The road in North Carolina where Karate for Christ International's headquarters is located
- b. The path that Jesus took to Galilee
- c. The Roman Road is a collection of verses in Paul's Epistle to the Romans that offers a clear and structured path to Jesus Christ
- d. The Roman Road is a mythological journey that ancient warriors had to travel before reaching manhood

18. David Sheram said the following about being an instructor:
- a. We must be the highest achieving student of our style and have many awards and titles to add to our resume before teaching a ministry class.
- b. Our goal in teaching is to be like the Master Teacher, Jesus Christ. A quality teacher must be Christ-like. The best training comes from modeling.
- c. It is best to follow how secular teachers teach because they know what they are doing and we can learn a great deal from them.
- d. Jesus would not have approved of martial arts training because of it's violence so we must be careful to teach non-violent ways.

19. Our students will become like us. How we stand, they will stand. How we punch, they will punch. How we move, they will move. How we act, they will act. How we exemplify Jesus in our families, dojangs, business ethics, and personal lives, they will want to be the same way. We should deliver what we believe to be the truth.
- a. True
- b. False

I- Intuitive

    N- (K)nowledgeable

S- Serious
T- Tentative
R- Reliable
U- Understanding
C- Creative
T- Tenacious
O- Organized
R- Responsible

20. The above acrostic by David Sheram is:
    a. True
    b. False

21. George Petrotta of Sunja Do explains the history of bowing in the martial arst in the following way (choose all that apply):
    a. Bowing in the orient is a way to worship your teacher and his dead ancestors
    b. Bowing in the orient is much like a hand shake in the West
    c. Bowing is a sign of respectful greeting
    d. Bowing is not the best way to show respect because you could be injured when taking your eye off your teacher or another student
    e. Bowing to another person is to indicate that you trust him enough to willingly take your eyes off of him

22. The use of different belt colors to signify rank was first introduced by:
    a. Dr. Kano
    b. Dr. Covington
    c. Dr. Petrotta
    d. Sun Tzu

23. There is honor in defeating a much weaker opponent.
    a. True
    b. False

24. According to George Petrotta, teaching basics does the following thing:
    a. It ensures that you do not forget them yourself
    b. Provides the foundation, like the cornerstones of a skyscraper
    c. Helps those students who don't learn fast to learn something
    d. None of the above

25. Free ways to promote your Martial Arts ministry could include the following (choose all that apply):
    a. Business cards with your name, class times and location distributed throughout the community

      b.   Fliers put in all locations with or without the permission of premise owners

      c.   Free lesson offers

      d.   Bulletin boards

      e.   Newspaper ads

26. David Dunn's martial arts ministry started out full of energy and stayed that way the whole time.
    a. True
    b. False

27. Running a martial arts ministry, according to David Dunn, is smoother than running a commercial school.
    a. True
    b. False

28. David Dunn's Karate for Christ ministry shows us the following (choose all that apply):
    a. If we are diligent and do not give up, we will see God's hand move in our classes
    b. Karate for Christ ministries are easy to run and never have problems
    c. It can be exhausting and seem unfruitful at times running a martial arts ministry
    d. The students almost never gain any insight to God from our efforts

29. Martial arts is a great tool to help ADD/ADHD students learn how to focus and apply themselves in life and school.
    a. True
    b. False

30. Martial arts instructors do not need to know if their students have ADD/ADHD or autism.
    a. True
    b. False

31. Martial arts instructors should keep the ADD/ADHD students in a separate class away from all other students.
    a. True
    b. False

32. ADD/ADHD student always need medication and you, as a martial arts instructor, should encourage parents to follow this path.

      a.   True
      b.   False

33. ADD/ADHD students have many desirable qualities that need to be harnessed and developed.
    a. True
    b. False

34. The type of learning that happens in a classroom setting is:
    a. Transformational
    b. Informational
    c. Constipational
    d. International

35. The type of learning that happens in the dojo/dojang is:
    a. Transformational
    b. Informational
    c. Constipational
    d. International

36. Chris Dewey explains that when we teach a child a skill, such as a kick, the child learns much more than just the kick, he also learns (choose all that apply):
    a. To keep his training partner safe while practicing a kick
    b. Body awareness
    c. That an inability to control his kick means less partners will want to train with him
    d. The reflexology of the kick

37. Evaluate the following statement by Daryl Covington: *One of the biggest negatives I hear about my own involvement and teaching of martial arts is that I am merely teaching people how to fight. In reality, I teach students so they do not have to fight.*
    a. True
    b. False

38. Evaluate the following statement by Daryl Covington: *There is not a crisis in our country in a spiritual manner. Three of four Americans do believe in absolute truth. We teach evolution and the children respond.*
    a. True
    b. False

39. There is never a place for meditation in the Christian martial arts ministry because of the Eastern influence that it brings in to class.
    a. True
    b. False

40. A great misconception many get is the idea that Christians are:
    a.   Not supposed to defend themselves
    b.   Supposed to defend themselves
    c.   Not good martial artists
    d.   None of the above

41. In the bible, God says Christians are not supposed to:
    a.   Be vigilantes and take revenge
    b.   Sit by and let people get away with things
    c.   Study fighting methods
    d.   None of the above

APPENDIX J: ASIA REACH SUPPORT DOCUMENTS

ARM / KFCI SUPPORT TEAM

ARM and KFCI are joining together not only to reach Asia with the Word of God but also to reach the youth of America through the KFCI schools. To that end, we have established a "support team prospective" that will provide the ARM team with the finances necessary to spread the gospel in Asia, give KFCI schools advertisement for their ministry, and provide individuals with the information they need to pray effectively for the spiritual needs in Asia. Please prayerfully consider which of the following teams God would have you to join to reach Asia for Him:

Foundational, Gold, Silver, or Precious Stones Support Team.

Now if any man build upon this foundation gold, silver, precious stones, wood, hay, stubble; Every man's work shall be made manifest: for the day shall declare it, because it shall be revealed by fire; and the fire shall try every man's work of what sort it is. 1Corinthians 3:12-13

☐FOUNDATION TEAM

Even the smallest amount of support is important in reaching Asia with the gospel. If a school owner, instructor, student, or individual is able to support ARM / KFCI by hosting an event, participating in a conference, or by any financial contribution, you will receive a certificate of appreciation from ARM / KFCI, as well as a KFCI Missions Support Team Patch to wear. For those that can support ARM for $10.00 a month or more, a Gold bar will be given to signify their dedication to monthly support of reaching Asia with the Word of God.

☐GOLD SUPPORT TEAM

This team is composed of school owners, instructors, students, and individuals that would agree to Support ARM for $25.00 per month or more.

ARM / KFCI Gold Support Team members would receive an ARM / KFCI Gold Support Team Certificate, a year's subscription (six issues) of the Asia Perspective Newsletter, a KFCI Missions Support Team Patch, and the ARM Gold Bar for monthly supporters.

☐ SILVER SUPPORT TEAM

This team is composed of school owners, instructors, students, and individuals that would agree to support ARM for $50.00 per month or more.

ARM / KFCI Silver Support Team members would receive an ARM / KFCI Silver Support Team Certificate, a year's subscription (six issues) of the Asia Perspective Newsletter, a KFCI Missions Support Team Patch, and the ARM Gold Bar for monthly supporters.

☐ DIAMOND SUPPORT TEAM

This team is composed of school owners, instructors, students, and individuals that would agree to support ARM for $75.00 per month.

ARM / KFCI Precious Stones Support Team members would receive an ARM / KFCI Precious Stones Support Team Certificate, a year's subscription (six issues) of the Asia Perspective Newsletter, a KFCI Missions Support Team Patch, the ARM Gold Bar Monthly Support Team Patch, and would have their name or the name of their school listed as a support team member on the ARM website.

☐WHAT NEXT

To join one of the support teams mentioned above you can do one of the following:

1. Make a copy of the support team contact form on the next page, check the box beside the support team you choose to join, fill out the contact information section and mail it to our support address shown below with your first month's gift

2. Or fill out our automated form found at http://www.asiareach.org/......

SUPPORT TEAM CONTACT FORM

☐ **Support Team** ($10 + month)
☐**Gold Support Team** ($25.00 + month)
☐**Silver Support Team** ($50.00 + month)
☐**Precious Stones Support Team** ($75.00 +)

Last Name:

School Name:

Home Address:

School Address:

Home Phone:

School Phone:

Work Phone:

Mobil Phone:

E-Mail:

APPENDIX K: ABOUT ASIA REACH MINISTRIES

Asia is the most populated and unreached continent in the world. Asia Reach Ministries purposes to get the Gospel to these billions of unreached people. As Bible believers, we are a ministry of and accountable to **Midland Baptist Church** Midland, Michigan. The purpose of this section of the book is to give you a clear understanding of the breadth and scope of Asia Reach Ministries, its partners, and its vision. The Members of Asia Reach Ministries / KFCI Missions team:

The Covington Family

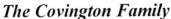

Daryl was saved in 1979. He was called into full time ministry while serving the United States Army in Iraq during Desert Storm. He participated in various ministries while attending Auburn University. After completing the Bachelor of Science in Biology, he enrolled a Master of Divinity program, and began pastoring at that same time. During his 10 years as a pastor, he went on to finish has Masters and Doctor of Ministry degrees, as well as a PhD in Asian Studies. He served as pastor of White Oak Baptist Church, North Carolina, until his call to missions in 2005. Brenda was saved in 1994. Since then, she has home-schooled our two daughters, Mikayla and Miriah (both of whom are saved), taught children?s Bible studies, both on the church and missions field, and participated in public ministry. After two trips to the Philippines with the Faulks, and a trip to Communist China with the Mongers, the Covingtons answered the Lord?s call to the mission field of Korea, and began ministering there in October of 2005. Dr. Covington also serves as the president of Karate for Christ International.

The Faulk Family

Tim and Michele Faulk both trusted Christ as their Saviour in March of 1985. The Faulks have both depth and breadth in ministry. Brother Tim is an excellent preacher and teacher of God's Word. Michele is also an excellent teacher to ladies and children. They are faithful witnesses to the lost and great encouragers to the saved. Brother Tim has had a hand in planting churches here in the US as well as in Asia since 1989. He started and pastored Grace Baptist Church in Mary Esther, FL until his call to missions in 1995. Michele has led ladies fellowships, has home schooled their four children, taught Christian school in the Philippines and ministered in a "common sense" medical way to the needy in Southeast Asia.

The Monger Family

Bobby was saved in 1989 and called into full-time service the next year. He served in various church ministries including Sunday school, church visitation, nursing home, and adult and juvenile prison ministries until his call to China in 1995. In China, Bobby has been faithful to minister to the lost even under harsh political restrictions and has aided in the placement of new missionary families to the field of China. Julie was saved in 1979. She takes an active part in the ministry by giving her testimony, helping in the Chinese print ministry, discipling Chinese Christian ladies, and home schooling their four children.

The Taylor Family

Hugh and Regina got saved in 1965 and 1978, respectively. They have over 25 years of diverse ministry experience in various churches in the US and overseas during military and missionary service. A gifted preacher and teacher, Hugh is also a skilled and effective leader; spanning differences in culture, age, language, and education levels to build teamwork and accomplish the mission. Regina is also a talented and proven teacher with ladies groups and children. She has taught in Christian schools in the US and overseas, as well as home schooling their three children.

The Locsin Family

Pastor Mario Locsin surrendered to preach soon after getting saved while still in high school. He earned his Bachelor of Theology from Baptist International Theological College in 1985 and his Bachelor of Bible from Open Bible College in 1998, both in Oton, Iloilo. Upon graduation he pastored First Independent Baptist Church of Wright in Wright, Tapaz, Capiz (1985-1987) and then New Testament Baptist Church in Trapiche, Iloilo (1987-1992). He pioneered and pastored Grace Gospel Baptist Church, Caumpang, General Santos City (1993-1998) and then served as Executive Dean of Open Bible College, Oton, Iloilo (1998-2002). Since 2002, he has pioneered and pastored Grace Gospel Baptist Church, Banilad, Cebu City. He also presently serves as the Philippines National Director for Asia Reach Ministries.

It has been said that every successful man has a woman behind him. Pastor Locsin acknowledges that his wife, Anamarie, is such a woman. She has been greatly used to partner with him in the ministry. Both of them were classmates in college and were married in 1986, a year after graduation. Those who know her can testify of how faithful, enthusiastic, and joyful she is in serving the Lord. She is a great soul winner, encourager, and a happy companion. She has taught children in kindergarten , and currently plays the organ and piano for the church. Anamarie is the mother of two children, Pepit (a girl) and Jes-jes (a boy).

Statement of Ministry for Asia Reach

Authority:

Our final authority is the Bible. We are a ministry of and accountable to Midland Baptist Church, Midland, Michigan.

Vision:

That every community of every country in Asia have a Bible-believing church so that every resident might have a gospel witness and every believer be grounded and settled in the truth.

Purpose:

Reach Asia with the Word of God.

Mission:

Minister in partnership as ambassadors for Christ throughout Asia that people might be reconciled to God and see the fellowship of the mystery of Christ as revealed in the Word of God.

Strategy:

- Evangelize the lost through preaching, personal relationships, literature distribution, and outreach Bible studies.
- Establish churches in urban and rural areas that are indigenously led, internally supported, and intentionally replicating.
- Educate the faithful with study aids, discipleship, conferences, courses, and seminars.
- Equip and empower ministers with resources, ministry capabilities, and encouragement.

Philosophy of Ministry:

Our ministry is to be patterned in principle and practice after that of the Apostle Paul. We are to follow Paul as he followed Christ. Therefore:

- We do what is right according to the Word and leadership of God.
- We walk and minister in grace, truth, and purpose.
- We seek to glorify God and edify others in partnership, and not to build personal or organizational empires.
- We minister as an expression of excellence with integrity and without extravagance.
- We maintain accountability to God, our partners, and our supporters.

Statement of Faith

We believe in the verbal-plenary inspiration and preservation of the scriptures. Deuteronomy 4:2, Psalm 12:6-7, Proverbs 3:5-6, and Revelation 22:18-19.

We believe in one true God, eternally existing in three persons: God the Father, God the Son, and God the Holy Spirit. Matthew 3:16, Acts 17:29, Romans 1:20, and Colossians 2:9.

We believe in the Lord Jesus Christ as virgin born, true God, and true man, as well as His impeccability, voluntary and substitutionary death, bodily resurrection, present advocacy, pre-tribulational rapture of the church, personal pre-millennial return, and 1,000-year reign. Matthew 1:25, I Thessalonians 4:13-18, I Timothy 2:5, I Timothy 3:16, I John 2:1, Revelation 19:11-18. We believe in the fall of man resulting in his death of spirit, nature of sin, and need of salvation. Genesis 3:6; Romans 3:10-18, 23; and Romans 6:23.

We believe that salvation is a free and everlasting gift of God entirely apart from man?s works. Every person is responsible to receive salvation by personal belief on the Lord Jesus Christ. Although every person can reject the gift of salvation by never believing on the Lord Jesus Christ, once salvation is accepted it can not be lost or rejected due to the sealing of the believer in the Body of Christ by the Holy Spirit. Romans 6:23, 11:6; Ephesians 1:13, 2:8-9, 4:30; and Titus 3:5-6.

We believe the Holy Spirit regenerates the believer, baptizing him into and sealing him in the Body of Christ. I Corinthians 12:13 and Titus 3:5.

We believe in eternal conscious bliss with the Lord Jesus Christ for the saved, and eternal conscious torment in hell for the unsaved. I Thessalonians 4:16-17, Philippians 3:20-21, and Mark 9:44, 46, and 48.

We recognize the Apostle Paul as Gods special example and pattern for the church and believe we are charged by God to follow Paul as he followed Christ. Romans 11:13, 15:15-21; I Corinthians 11:1; Philippians 3:17; and I Timothy 1:16.

We believe in a strong local church and missionary emphasis. We believe every believer has the responsibility to get the gospel to every person in every generation. All can not physically go to a foreign field, but all can be directly involved in worldwide evangelization by prayer, finances, and encouragement, as well as giving the gospel to the lost who live nearby. Acts 13:47 and Romans 10:14-17.

ASIA REACH MINISTRIES

P.O. BOX 12

SANFORD, MI 48657

989-687-6999

LaVergne, TN USA
26 September 2010
198508LV00002B/12/A